Theodore Roosevelt, Conservation, and the 1908 Governors' Conference

Library of Presidential Rhetoric

Theodore Roosevelt, Conservation, and the 1908 Governors' Conference

Leroy G. Dorsey

Texas A&M University Press

COLLEGE STATION

First edition

This paper meets the requirements of ANSI/NISO Z39.48-1992
(Permanence of Paper).
Binding materials have been chosen for durability.
Manufactured in the United States of America

LIBRARY OF CONGRESS CATALOGING-IN-PUBLICATION DATA

Names: Dorsey, Leroy G., 1959– author.
Title: Theodore Roosevelt, conservation, and the 1908 Governors' Conference / Leroy G. Dorsey.
Other titles: Library of presidential rhetoric.
Description: First edition. | College Station : Texas A&M University Press, [2016] | ?2016 | Series: Library of presidential rhetoric | Includes bibliographical references and index.
Identifiers: LCCN 2015044698| ISBN 9781623493998 (pbk. : alk. paper) | ISBN 9781623494001 (ebook)
Subjects: LCSH: Roosevelt, Theodore, 1858-1919—Oratory. | Roosevelt, Theodore, 1858-1919—Political and social views. | Presidents—United States—Messages—History—20th century. | Presidents—United States—Language—History—20th century. | Political oratory—United States—History—20th century. | Rhetoric—Political aspects—United States—History—20th century. | Speeches, addresses, etc., American—History and criticism. | Communication in politics—United States—History—20th century. | Conservation of natural resources—United States—Congresses—History—20th century. | Communication in conservation of natural resources—United States—History—20th century. | Conservation of natural resources—Government policy—United States—History—20th century. | Conference of Governors (1st : 1908 : Washington, D.C.)
Classification: LCC E757 .D666 2016 | DDC 973.91/1092—dc23 LC record available at http://lccn.loc.gov/2015044698

For Adam and Alicia

Contents

Acknowledgments

I have been writing about the rhetoric of Theodore Roosevelt for quite some time. As a result, I have benefitted from many colleagues' advice along the way. So, in a real sense, this book is a culmination of the fine insights I have received over the years from incredibly thoughtful people. Two in particular I'd like to mention are Martin J. Medhurst and Mary Stuckey; their work has been very influential in my own writing on the rhetorical nature of the presidency.

Next, I would like to thank both Mary Lenn Dixon and Jay Dew at Texas A&M University Press. Mary Lenn, as the previous editor-in-chief, ran into me at a National Communication Association conference in 2013, and we talked about this very project. She helped me think it through in its earliest incarnation. Although she retired right before I submitted the proposal, Jay—as a new editor—helped me tremendously with his insight and encouragement. The entire administrative staff at Texas A&M University Press have all been extremely helpful.

I am also grateful for the two reviewers' critiques. They both helped me see things—in grand terms and more nuanced ones—that undoubtedly made the book better. Any errors, however, are all mine.

Finally, I'm grateful for the support I receive from my wife, Alicia, and my son, Adam. They mean everything to me.

Theodore Roosevelt, Conservation, and the 1908 Governors' Conference

Theodore Roosevelt's Opening Address at the Governors' Conference, May 13, 1908

Governors of the several States; and Gentlemen:

I welcome you to this Conference at the White House. You have come hither at my request, so that we may join together to consider the question of the conservation and use of the great fundamental sources of wealth of this Nation.

So vital is this question, that for the first time in our history the chief executive officers of the States separately, and of the States together forming the Nation, have met to consider it. It is the chief material question that confronts us, second only—and second always—to the great fundamental questions of morality. [Applause]

With the governors come men from each State chosen for their special acquaintance with the terms of the problem that is before us. Among them are experts in natural resources and representatives of national organizations concerned in the development and use of these resources; the Senators and Representatives in Congress; the Supreme Court, the Cabinet, and the Inland Waterways Commission have likewise been invited to the Conference, which is therefore national in a peculiar sense.

This Conference on the conservation of natural resources is in effect a meeting of the representatives of all the people of the United States called to consider the weightiest problem now before the Nation; and the occasion for the meeting lies in the fact that the natural resources of our country are in danger of exhaustion if we permit the old wasteful methods of exploiting them longer to continue.

With the rise of peoples from savagery to civilization, and with the consequent growth in the extent and variety of the needs of the average man, there comes a steadily increasing growth of the amount demanded by this average man from the actual resources of the country. And yet, rather curiously, at the same time that there comes that increase in what the average man demands from the resources, he is apt to grow to lose the sense of his dependence upon nature. He lives in big cities. He deals in industries that do not bring him in close touch with nature. He does not realize the demands he is making upon nature. For instance, he finds, as he has found before in many parts of this country, that it is cheaper to build his house of concrete than of wood, learning in this way only that he has allowed the woods to become exhausted. That is happening, as you know, in parts of this country at this very time.

Savages, and very primitive peoples generally, concern themselves only with superficial natural resources; with those which they obtain from the actual surface of the ground. As peoples become a little less primitive, their industries, although in a rude manner, are extended to resources below the surface; then, with what we call civilization and the extension of knowledge, more resources come into use, industries are multiplied, and foresight begins to become a necessary and prominent factor in life. Crops are cultivated; animals are domesticated; and metals are mastered.

We cannot do any of these things without foresight, and we can not, when the nation becomes fully civilized and very rich, continue to be civilized and rich unless the nation shows more foresight than we are showing at this moment as a nation. [Applause]

Every step of the progress of mankind is marked by the discovery and use of natural resources previously unused. Without such progressive knowledge and utilization of natural resources, population could not grow, nor industries multiply, nor the hidden wealth of the earth be developed for the benefit of mankind.

From the first beginnings of civilization, on the banks of the Nile and the Euphrates, the industrial progress of the world has gone on slowly, with occasional set-backs, but on the whole steadily, through tens of centuries to the present day.

It never does advance by jumps, gentlemen. It always goes slowly. There are occasional set-backs, but on the whole it goes steadily.

But of late the rapidity of the process has increased at such a rate that more space has been actually covered during the century and a quarter occupied by our national life than during the preceding six thousand years that take us back to the earliest monuments of Egypt, to the earliest cities of the Babylonian plain.

Now, I ask you to think what that means; and I am speaking with historic literalness. In the development, the use, and therefore the exhaustion of certain of the natural resources, the progress has been more rapid in the past century and a quarter than during all preceding time of which we have record.

When the founders of this nation met at Independence Hall in Philadelphia, the conditions of commerce had not fundamentally changed from what they were when the Phoenician keels first furrowed the lonely waters of the Mediterranean.

You turn to Homer—some of you did in your school days, even if you do not now [laughter]—and you will see that he spoke, not of the Mediterranean but of one corner of the Egean only, as a limitless waste of water which no one had traversed. There is now no nook of the earth that we are not searching.

When our forefathers met in Independence Hall, the differences were those of degrees, not of kind, and they were not in all cases even those of degree. Mining was carried on fundamentally as it had been carried on by the Pharaohs in the countries adjacent to the Red Sea. Explorers now-a-days by the shores of the Red Sea strike countries that they call new, but they find in them mines, with sculptures of the Pharaohs, showing that those mines were worked out and exhausted thousands of years before the Christian era.

In 1776 the wares of the merchants of Boston, of Charleston, like the wares of the merchants of Nineveh and Sidon, if they went by water, were carried by boats propelled by sails or oars; if they went by land were carried in wagons drawn by beasts of draft or in packs on the backs of beasts of burden. The ships that crossed the high seas were better than the ships that three thousand years before crossed the Egean, but they were of the same type, after all—they were wooden ships propelled by sails. There the difference was one of degree in our favor. On shore the difference was one of degree against us, for on land the roads, at the end of the eighteenth century, when this country became a nation, were not as good as the roads of the Roman Empire, while the service of the posts, at any rate prior to the days of Benjamin Franklin, was probably inferior. In the previous eighteen hundred years there had been a retrogression in roads and in postal service.

In Washington's time anthracite coal was known only as a useless black stone; and the great fields of bituminous coal were undiscovered. As steam was unknown, the use of coal for power production was undreamed of. Water was practically the only source of power, saved the labor of men and animals; and this power was used only in the most primitive fashion. But a few small iron deposits had been found in this country, and the use of iron by our countrymen was very small. Wood was practically the only fuel, and what lumber was sawed was consumed locally, while the forests were regarded chiefly as obstructions to settlement and cultivation. The man who cut down a tree was held to have conferred a service upon his fellows.

Such was the degree of progress to which civilized mankind had attained when this nation began its career. It is almost impossible for us in this day to realize how little our Revolutionary ancestors knew of the great store of natural resources whose discovery and use have been such vital factors in the growth and greatness of this Nation, and how little they required to take from this store in order to satisfy their needs.

Since then our knowledge and use of the resources of the present territory of the United States have increased a hundred-fold. Indeed, the growth of this Nation by leaps and bounds makes one of the most striking and important chapters in the history of the world. Its growth has been due to the rapid development, and alas that it should be said to the rapid destruction, of our natural resources. Nature has supplied to us in the United States, and still supplies to us, more kinds of resources in a more lavish degree than has ever been the case at any other time or with any other people. Our position in the world has been attained by the extent and thoroughness of the control we have achieved over nature; but we are more, and not less, dependent upon what she furnishes than at any previous time of history since the days of primitive man.

Yet our fathers, though they knew so little of the resources of the country, exercised a wise forethought in reference thereto. Washington clearly saw that the perpetuity of the States could only be secured by union, and that the only feasible basis of union was an economic one; in other words, that it must be based on the development and use of their natural resources. Accordingly, he helped to outline a scheme of commercial development, and by his influence an interstate waterways commission was appointed by Virginia and Maryland.

It met near where we are now meeting, in Alexandria, adjourned to Mount Vernon, and took up the consideration of interstate commerce by the only means then available, that of water; and the trouble we have since had with the railways has been mainly due to the fact that naturally our forefathers could not divine that the iron road would become the interstate and international highway, instead of the old route by water. Further conferences were arranged, first at Annapolis, and then at Philadelphia. It was in Philadelphia that the representatives of all the States met for what was in its original conception merely a waterways conference; but when they had closed their deliberations the outcome was the Constitution which made the States into a nation. [Applause]

The Constitution of the United States thus grew in large part out of the necessity for united action in the wise use of one of our natural resources. The wise use of all of our natural resources, which are our national resources as well, is the great material question of today. I have asked you to come together now because the enormous consumption of these resources, and the threat of imminent exhaustion of some of them, due to reckless and wasteful use, once more calls for common effort, common action.

We want to take action that will prevent the advent of a woodless age, and defer as long as possible the advent of an ironless age. [Applause]

Since the days when the Constitution was adopted, steam and electricity have revolutionized the industrial world. Nowhere has the revolution been so great as in our own country. The discovery and utilization of mineral fuels and alloys have given us the lead over all other nations in the production of steel. The discovery and utilization of coal and iron have given us our railways, and have led to such industrial development as has never before been seen. The vast wealth of lumber in our forests, the riches of our soils and mines, the discovery of gold and mineral oils, combined with the efficiency of our transportation, have made the conditions of our life unparalleled in comfort and convenience.

A great many of these things are truisms. Much of what I say is so familiar to us that it seems commonplace to repeat it; but familiar though it is, I do not think as a nation we understand what its real bearing is. It is so familiar that we disregard it. [Applause]

The steadily increasing drain on these natural resources has promoted to an extraordinary degree the complexity of our industrial and social life. Moreover, this unexampled development has had a determining effect upon the character and opinions of our people. The demand for efficiency in the great task has given us vigor, effectiveness, decision, and power, and a capacity for achievement which in its own lines has never yet been matched. [Applause] So great and so rapid has been our material growth that there has been a tendency to lag behind in spiritual and moral growth [laughter and applause]; but that is not the subject upon which I speak to you today.

Disregarding for the moment the question of moral purpose, it is safe to say that the prosperity of our people depends directly on the energy and intelligence with which our natural resources are used. It is equally clear that these resources are the final basis of national power and perpetuity. Finally, it is ominously evident that these resources are in the course of rapid exhaustion.

This Nation began with the belief that its landed possessions were illimitable and capable of supporting all the people who might care to make our country their home; but already the limit of unsettled land is in sight, and indeed but little land fitted for agriculture now remains unoccupied save what can be reclaimed by irrigation and drainage—a subject with which this Conference is partly to deal. We began with an unapproached heritage of forests; more than half of the timber is gone. We began with coal fields more extensive than those of any other nation and with iron ores regarded as inexhaustible, and many experts now declare that the end of both iron and coal is in sight.

The mere increase in our consumption of coal during 1907 over 1906 exceeded the total consumption in 1876, the Centennial year. This is a striking fact: Thirty years went by, and the mere surplus of use of one year over the preceding year exceeded all that was used in 1876—and we thought we were pretty busy people even then. The enormous stores of mineral oil and gas are largely gone; and those Governors who have in their States cities built up by natural gas, where the natural gas has since been exhausted, can tell us something of what that means. Our natural waterways are not gone, but they have been so injured by neglect, and by the division of responsibility and utter lack of system in dealing with them, that there is less navigation on them now than there was fifty years ago. Finally, we began with soils of unexampled fertility, and we have so impoverished them by injudicious use and by failing to check erosion that their crop-producing power is diminishing instead of increasing. In a word, we have thoughtlessly, and to a large degree unnecessarily, diminished the resources upon which not only our prosperity but the prosperity of our children and our children's children must always depend.

We have become great in a material sense because of the lavish use of our resources, and we have just reason to be proud of our growth. But the time has come to inquire seriously what will happen when our forests are gone, when the coal, the iron, the oil, and the gas are exhausted, when the soils shall have been still further impoverished and washed into the streams, polluting the rivers, denuding the fields, and obstructing navigation. These questions do not relate only to the next century or to the next generation. One distinguishing characteristic of really civilized men is foresight; we have to, as a nation, exercise foresight for this nation in the future; and if we do not exercise that foresight, dark will be the future! [Applause] We should exercise foresight now, as the ordinarily prudent man exercises foresight in conserving and wisely using the property which contains the assurance of well-being for himself and his children. We want to see a man own his farm rather than rent it, because we want to see it an object to him to transfer it in better order to his children. We want to see him exercise forethought for the next generation. We need to exercise it in some fashion ourselves as a nation for the next generation.

The natural resources I have enumerated can be divided into two sharply distinguished classes accordingly as they are or are not capable of renewal.

Mines if used must necessarily be exhausted. The minerals do not and can not renew themselves. Therefore in dealing with the coal, the oil, the gas, the iron, the metals generally, all that we can do is to try to see that they are wisely used. The exhaustion is certain to come in time. We can trust that it will be deferred long enough to enable the extraordinarily inventive genius of our people to devise means and methods for more or less adequately replacing what is lost; but the exhaustion is sure to come.

The second class of resources consists of those which can not only be used in such manner as to leave them undiminished for our children, but can actually be improved by wise use. The soil, the forests, the waterways come in this category. Every one knows that a really good farmer leaves his farm more valuable at the end of his life than it was when he first took hold of it. So with the waterways. So with the forests. In dealing with mineral resources, man is able to improve on nature only by putting the resources to a beneficial use which in the end exhausts them; but in dealing with the soil and its products man can improve on nature by compelling the resources to renew and even reconstruct themselves in such manner as to serve increasingly beneficial uses—while the living waters can be so controlled as to multiply their benefits.

Neither the primitive man nor the pioneer was aware of any duty to posterity in dealing with the renewable resources. When the American settler felled the forests, he felt that there was plenty of forest left for the sons who came after him. When he exhausted the soil of his farm, he felt that his son could go West and take up another. The Kentuckian or the Ohioan felled the forest and expected his son to move west and fell other forests on the banks of the Mississippi; the Georgian exhausted his farm and moved into Alabama or to the mouth of the Yazoo to take another. So it was with his immediate successors. When the soil-wash from the farmer's field choked the neighboring river, the only thought was to use the railway rather than the boats to move produce and supplies. That was so up to the generation that preceded ours.

Now all this is changed. On the average the son of the farmer of today must make his living on his father's farm. There is no difficulty in doing this if the father will exercise wisdom. No wise use of a farm exhausts its fertility. So with the forests. We are over the verge of a timber famine in this country, and it is unpardonable for the Nation or the States to permit any further cutting of our timber save in accordance with a system which will provide that the next generation shall see the timber increased instead of diminished. [Applause]

Just let me interject one word as to a particular type of folly of which it ought not to be necessary to speak. We stop wasteful cutting of timber; that of course makes a slight shortage at the moment. To avoid that slight shortage at the moment, there are certain people so foolish that they will incur absolute shortage in the future, and they are willing to stop all attempts to conserve the forests, because of course by wastefully using them at the moment we can for a year or two provide against any lack of wood. That is like providing for the farmer's family to live sumptuously on the flesh of the milch cow. [Laughter] Any farmer can live pretty well for a year if he is content not to live at all the year after. [Laughter and applause]

We can, moreover, add enormous tracts of the most valuable possible agricultural land to the national domain by irrigation in the arid and semi-arid regions, and by drainage of great tracts of swamp land in the humid regions. We can enormously increase our transportation facilities by the canalization of our rivers so as to complete a great system of waterways on the Pacific, Atlantic, and Gulf coasts, and in the Mississippi Valley, from the Great Plains to the Alleghenies, and from the northern lakes to the mouth of the mighty Father of Waters. But all these various uses of our natural resources are so closely connected that they should be coordinated, and should be treated as part of one coherent plan and not in haphazard and piecemeal fashion.

It is largely because of this that I appointed the Waterways Commission last year, and that I sought to perpetuate its work. There are members of the coordinate branch present. The reason this meeting takes place is because we had that waterways commission last year. I had to prosecute the work by myself. I have asked Congress to pass a bill giving some small sum of money for the perpetuation of that Commission. If Congress does not act, I will perpetuate the Commission anyway [Great applause], but of course it is a great deal better that Congress should act [Applause]; it enables the work to be more effectively done. I hope there will be action. But the Commission will go ahead.

I wish to take this opportunity to express in heartiest fashion my acknowledgment to all the members of the Commission. At great personal sacrifice of time and effort they have rendered a service to the public for which we can not be too grateful. Especial credit is due to the initiative, the energy, the devotion to duty, and the farsightedness of Gifford Pinchot [Great applause], to whom we owe so much of the progress we have already made in handling this matter of the coordination and conservation of natural resources. If it had not been for him this convention neither would nor could have been called.

We are coming to recognize as never before the right of the Nation to guard its own future in the essential matter of natural resources. In the past we have admitted the right of the individual to injure the future of the Republic for his own present profit. In fact there has been a good deal of a demand for unrestricted individualism, for the right of the individual to injure the future of all of us for his own temporary and immediate profit. The time has come for a change. As a people we have the right and the duty, second to none other but the right and duty of obeying the moral law, of requiring and doing justice, to protect ourselves and our children against the wasteful development of our natural resources, whether that waste is caused by the actual destruction of such resources or by making them impossible of development hereafter.

Any right thinking father earnestly desires and strives to leave his son both an untarnished name and a reasonable equipment for the struggle of life. So this Nation as a whole should earnestly desire and strive to leave to the next generation the national honor unstained and the national resources unexhausted. There are signs that both the Nation and the States are waking to a realization of this great truth—On March 10, 1908, the Supreme Court of Maine rendered an exceedingly important judicial decision. This opinion was rendered in response to questions as to the right of the Legislature to restrict the cutting of trees on private land for the prevention of droughts and floods, the preservation of the natural water supply, and the prevention of the erosion of such lands, and the consequent filling up of rivers, ponds, and lakes. The forests and water power of Maine constitute the larger part of her wealth and form the basis of her industrial life, and the question submitted by the Maine Senate to the Supreme Court and the answer of the Supreme Court alike bear testimony to the wisdom of the people of Maine, and clearly define a policy of conservation of natural resources, the adoption of which is of vital importance not merely to Maine but to the whole country. [Applause]

Such a policy will preserve soil, forests, water power as a heritage for the children and the children's children of the men and women of this generation; for any enactment that provides for the wise utilization of the forests, whether in public or private ownership, and for the conservation of the water resources of the country, must necessarily be legislation that will promote both private and public welfare; for flood prevention, water-power development, preservation of the soil, and improvement of navigable rivers are all promoted by such a policy of forest conservation.

The opinion of the Maine Supreme Bench sets forth unequivocally the principle that the property rights of the individual are subordinate to the rights of the community, and especially that the waste of wild timber land derived originally from the State, involving as it would the impoverishment of the State and its People and thereby defeating a great purpose of government, may properly be prevented by State restrictions.

The Court says that there are two reasons why the right of the public to control and limit the use of private property is peculiarly applicable to property in land:

First, such property is not the result of productive labor, but is derived solely from the State itself, the original owner; second, the amount of land being incapable of increase, if the owners of large tracts can waste them at will without State restriction, the State and its people may be helplessly impoverished and one great purpose of government defeated. . . . We do not think the proposed legislation would operate to "take" private property within the inhibition of the Constitution. While it might restrict the owner of wild and uncultivated lands in his use of them, might delay his taking some of the product, might delay his anticipated profits and even thereby might cause him some loss of profit, it would nevertheless leave him his lands, their product and increase, untouched, and without diminution of title, estate, or quantity. He would still have large measure of control and large opportunity to realize values. He might suffer delay but not deprivation. . . . The proposed legislation . . . would be within the legislative power and would not operate as a taking of private property for which compensation must be made.

The Court of Errors and Appeals of New Jersey has adopted a similar view, which has recently been sustained by the Supreme Court of the United States. In delivering the opinion of the Court on April 6, 1908, Mr. Justice Holmes said:

> The State as quasi sovereign and representative of the interests of the public has a standing in court to protect the atmosphere, the water, and the forests within its territory, irrespective of the assent or dissent of the private owners of the land most immediately concerned. . . . It appears to us that few public interests are more obvious, indisputable, and independent of particular theory than the interest of the public of a State to maintain the rivers that are wholly within it substantially undiminished, except by such drafts upon them as the guardian of the public welfare may permit for the purpose of turning them to a more perfect use.

[Applause]

> This public interest is omnipresent wherever there is a State, and grows more pressing as population grows.

Not as a dictum of law, which I cannot make, but as a dictum of moral, I wish to say that this applies to more than the forests and streams. [Laughter and applause] The learned Justice proceeds:

> We are of opinion, further, that the constitutional power of the State to insist that its natural advantages shall remain unimpaired by its citizens is not dependent upon any nice estimate of the extent of present use or speculation as to future needs. The legal conception of the necessary is apt to be confined to somewhat rudimentary wants, and there are benefits from a great river that might escape a lawyer's view.

[Laughter] I have simply quoted. [Laughter]

> But the State is not required to submit even to an esthetic analysis. Any analysis may be inadequate. It finds itself in possession of what all admit to be a great public good, and want it has it may keep and give no one a reason for its will.

These decisions reach the root of the idea of conservation of our resources in the interests of our people.

Finally, let us remember that the conservation of our natural resources, though the gravest problem of today, is yet but part of another and greater problem to which this Nation is not yet awake, but to which it will awake in time, and with which it must hereafter grapple if it is to live—the problem of national efficiency, the patriotic duty of insuring the safety and continuance of the Nation. [Applause]. When the People of the United States consciously undertake to raise themselves as citizens, and the Nation and the States in their several spheres, to the highest pitch of excellence in private, State, and national life, and to do this because it is the first of all the duties of true patriotism, then and not till then the future of this Nation, in quality and in time, will be assured. [Great applause]

One

Theodore Roosevelt and the Politics of Conservation

During his lifetime, Theodore Roosevelt was shocked at the wholesale destruction of trees, land, animals, and water resources. So he entered the presidency hell-bent on awakening the citizenry to the need for conservation and instituting change in the nation's environmental policies. Unquestionably, he faced overwhelming opposition from several quarters. The general public seemed disinterested in protecting the environment.[1] For those who did want to protect nature, some saw it as a godly obligation and clashed with others who saw it as scientific and managerial puzzle to solve.[2] Congress, having embraced a laissez-faire attitude that saw little interest in making fundamental changes to society, was thunderstruck by Roosevelt's determination to do just that. Legislators largely appeared to come down into two camps: those like Sen. William Clark dismissed conservation as a means to ensure the future, stating, "Those who succeed us can well take care of themselves;" or those like Rep. Herschel Hogg who ridiculed conservation as the province of "google-eyed, bandy-legged dudes from the East and sad-eyed, absent-minded professors and bugologists."[3] As a result, Congress resisted Roosevelt from the beginning on conservation and particularly went out of its way to impede his agenda in his second term. The president had been so aggressive on this issue, Douglas Brinkley noted, that businessmen openly hoped Roosevelt would die in "some godforsaken African port" when he talked about going on safari at the end of his presidency.[4]

Despite the forces arrayed against him during his tenure in the White House from 1901 to 1909, President Roosevelt took unprecedented steps to safeguard the environment. Over the course of those eight years, he established five national parks including ones at Crater Lake in Oregon and Mesa Verde in Colorado; four big game preserves in places such as Oklahoma and Arizona; fifty-one bird refuges in over a dozen states and territories; almost twenty national monuments including the Grand Canyon in Arizona, Mount Olympus in Washington, and Devil's Tower in Wyoming; and created 150 national forests across millions of acres in the United States.[5] The crown jewel of the national park system—Yellowstone—commemorated the president by naming the northern entrance archway and a camp area after him.[6] The National Park Service even identified Roosevelt as the country's first "conservation president."[7] Perhaps more important than those milestones, he changed attitudes about conservation and affirmed the federal government's authority over the environment.

It seems hard to imagine a moment in time when politicians and the public did not understand the concept of conservation, particularly given its ubiquitous discussion now by policymakers, pundits, private citizens, and Hollywood personalities.[8] The pivotal moment during Roosevelt's era when conservation went from being undefined, if not outright dismissed as an important topic in American culture, to being embraced as a meaningful national initiative, constitutes the focus of this book.

Specifically, this book centers on the unique rhetorical event most responsible for that moment of enlightenment. On May 13–15, 1908, President Roosevelt held an unprecedented conference. He invited all the states' governors and hundreds of representatives from business, education, government, science, media, and private organizations to the White House to hear him and others articulate a comprehensive plan to conserve the nation's resources, designate the parties responsible for the development and execution of that plan, and to illuminate the overarching stakes facing the nation if inaction on this matter continued. This Governors' Conference included Roosevelt's masterful opening speech that rhetorically positioned conservation in a way that reassessed America's past actions and presaged its possible future if nature was not saved. The event riveted the nation's attention and led to profound changes in American attitudes about conservation.

While the Library of Presidential Rhetoric Series asks authors to focus on one significant speech text by a chief executive, I expanded that focus by imagining the Governors' Conference itself as a text. Analyzing the discourse surrounding the organization of the conference, the rhetoric during and after the event including Roosevelt's speech, and how that august occasion showcased one of the president's most important speeches, provides greater insight into the process of presidential persuasion.

Some critics, however, have questioned the impact of the president's speech and the conference. Conservation scholar Frank Smith noted that

Roosevelt decided to use his speech at the Conference to generate support among legislators for his second-term project, the Inland Waterways Commission. That organization had generated a number of recommendations that the president wanted enacted into law but had been blocked by Congress. Smith concluded that the president's speech "changed few votes."[9] Environmental historian Samuel Hays admitted some inconsequential success because of the speech but said it proved to be no "big stick" to move Congress—in fact, the conference seemed to enrage House and Senate members even further.[10]

For some political scientists, a president's tendency to make speeches to popular audiences as a way to influence lawmakers represented an ill-informed path. Jeffrey Tulis took the position that Roosevelt's frequent attempts to "go over the heads of Congress" by appealing to the public—what Tulis labeled as the "rhetorical presidency"—ranked as an egregious offense. According to Tulis, Roosevelt used his "bully pulpit" as a pretense for preserving the nation's well-being while employing "demagoguery" and "blatant appeals to passion," tactics the Founding Fathers abhorred.[11] Gary Gregg observed that this more popular form of leadership rendered the constitutional system untenable. "Representation through rhetorical appeals has the effect of simplifying representative government. . . . Congress thereby is delegitimized to the same degree as the president claims primacy in providing representation."[12] Samuel Kernell believed Roosevelt hedged his bet in "going public" by commanding a still-new mass media to provide him with positive coverage that he dictated. By strong-arming the press, the president strategically silenced a potential check on his popular discourse.[13] Ironically, noted presidential scholar George Edwards looked with dismay at a president's use of popular rhetoric for a different reason. For him, a rhetorical presidency failed to matter. "It is one thing to go public," Edwards surmised, but "It is something quite different to succeed in moving public opinion." He concluded that presidents almost always fail when they leapfrog Congress seeking to gain support directly from the public.[14]

Such scholars who bemoaned a president's use of "popular rhetoric" to "go over the heads of Congress" expressed their desire to believe in a golden age when presidents shunned the public, thereby ensuring constitutional integrity between the executive and legislative branches. Their position, while interesting, perpetuated a misconception at several levels. First, the presidency has always been rhetorical. Several scholars in *The Presidency and Rhetorical Leadership* demonstrated how presidents as early as George Washington engaged in public behaviors that supposedly began with Theodore Roosevelt's rhetorical presidency.[15] Contributors to *Before the Rhetorical Presidency* likewise identified the "popular rhetoric" of Roosevelt's predecessors, ranging from Martin Van Buren to William McKinley. Second, as Martin J. Medhurst articulated, the original conception of a rhetorical presidency rested on several erroneous ideas about rhetoric. Scholars like Tulis conceived presidential rhetoric as only spoken, to the general public, about policy issues, which would subvert the ability of Congress to deliberate thoughtfully and fully. Medhurst dismissed the restrictive nature of that position, arguing that presidential rhetoric has a multitude of forms and purposes for differing audiences on differing occasions.[16] Third, limiting the rhetorical presidency just to a president's spoken discourse masks the notion that a chief executive can privately lead others to engage their rhetorical power for their own audiences on his behalf. Finally, whether a rhetorical president gains public support *in a measurable way* misses the more nuanced point: if his opponents believe that he might gain that public support with his "popular rhetoric," they might be more willing to negotiate with him.

The function and power of rhetoric has been a scholarly subject of study for centuries; the list of scholars grappling with it is too long to address here.[17] But twentieth century literary and rhetorical theorist Kenneth Burke offered a definition that encapsulated the modern understanding of rhetoric: the "use of language as a symbolic means of inducing cooperation in beings that by nature respond to symbols." Rhetoric represents an art that exists apart from the "realm of strictly true-or-false propositions" as dictated by science.[18] By Burke's definition, rhetorical acts involve probable outcomes based on those esoteric elements of life—human feelings—that are not knowable by precise scientific study as to how they will definitively impact decision-making.

Thus, presidents using rhetoric do not only deal with overt instances of changing public opinion about a particular piece of legislation, Kathleen Jamieson might say, but with less defined circumstances that may involve the empowerment of people to control their destiny across a varied number of dimensions.[19] It bears repeating: the presidency has always been rhetorical in the broadest sense of that term.

The dismissal of Roosevelt's speech specifically, and presidential appeals to popular audiences in general, also stems from what some people consider an apparent disconnect between rhetoric and reality. Putting aside the superficial notion that rhetoric is an art of illusion—to make fantasy appear real—the political gap between rhetoric and reality seems to come from the expectation that rhetoric can set and reset public opinion in some kind of instantaneous, all-or-nothing manner, with long-lasting effects that are evident in the moment of a president's use of that rhetoric. That bar is too unreasonable and ultimately unproductive for understanding rhetoric's potential to shape a way of life.

As this book will demonstrate, President Roosevelt's attempt to engage the public interest in conservation through the Governors' Conference, and to confirm the federal government's authority over business leaders and legislators in safeguarding the environment, involved a months-long campaign spanning multiple modes of interaction and advocates alike. In other words, the concept of the rhetorical presidency, as originally conceived by Tulis and others, lacks the flexibility to explain real-world uses of presidential rhetoric.

Instances of Roosevelt exercising his rhetorical ability should not be simply dismissed as abuses of presidential power. Such instances provide insight into how he "gained power while both reinforcing the political hierarchies . . . and discussing those hierarchies in democratic language." Mary Stuckey's assessment of President Roosevelt addressing the 1906 Brownsville Raid, for example, demonstrated that a rhetorical presidency involved more than "going over the heads of Congress" about some specific piece of legislation. The president's fight with Congress following his abrupt dismissal of a battalion of African American soldiers that he believed had acted dishonorably, and his subsequent defense of his actions, served to establish Roosevelt's "interpretive dominance" in matters related to cultural and institutional power. According to Stuckey, the president used several messages to the Senate to make his case about Brownsville, a case that gave him the opportunity to argue about race from "matters of principle, not politics," as he identified himself as an impartial commander in chief who made fair decisions based on the "importance of institutional rather than personal influences." Employing this rhetorical tactic allowed him to "associate himself" with and to affirm the "ethos of the presidency while associating the presidency with values integral [to] the nation's civic identity."[20]

Roosevelt likewise sought "interpretative dominance" in matters of conservation, particularly in affirming the social and economic need to protect the environment, and to confirm his right and the federal government's authority to oversee that protection. To that end, he attempted to rehabilitate his flagging personal reputation by associating himself more closely with a presidential institution that he rhetorically constructed as the unbiased and unquestioned steward of the nation's natural resources.

UNDERSTANDING ROOSEVELT AS A CONSERVATION PRESIDENT

The general warning about the ineffectuality of presidential popular discourse and the specific denunciations of Roosevelt's speech and the conference aside, his conservation rhetoric has been the subject of study. It remains surprising, though, that the "father of conservation" has not garnered more attention for his rhetorical efforts. Biographies on Theodore Roosevelt abound. But historical works about his life tend to breeze past his conservation efforts. Significant treatises on Roosevelt's life by esteemed historians such as H. W. Brands, Edmund Morris, and Doris Kearns Goodwin each spend a handful of pages describing the president's successes and battles, but provide little to no attention to the Governors' Conference itself. Even the works devoted solely to the president's environmental passion and politics, such as those by Paul Cutright and Douglas Brinkley, only spend a few pages chronicling the conference's events and even less time on the dynamics of the president's speech.[21] While useful, these primarily historical accounts do not engage in illuminating the strategic choices Roosevelt made in an attempt to guide audiences' acceptance of the importance of conservation and the federal government's role in managing that importance. He attempted to shape the world around him and, as James White might say, made "character and community—and motive, value, reason, social structure, everything . . . real in performances of language."[22]

Roosevelt's conservation discourse—his "performances of language"—has garnered some rhetorical attention. I have argued that Roosevelt used a number of strategies over time to appeal to public interest about the environment. For example, Roosevelt attempted to rally public support for conservation by invoking a myth to re-conceptualize the meaning of the American farmer. The "Frontier Myth" had long positioned pioneers as conquerors, heralding their destruction of the environment as a symbol of their heroics. In retelling that myth, Roosevelt lauded the real hero of the nation's origin, the yeoman farmer, whose tireless work to use nature wisely—rather than simply destroy it—symbolized true progress. The president also attempted to connect the protection of the environment to a civil religious construct that saw him preach about God's bestowal of nature's bounty on the American people—a people who had sinned with their assault on nature and whose souls now needed saving. "This civil religious construct of God, sin, and redemption," I argued, allowed "Roosevelt to link the environment and conservation to morality and, in turn, to the institutional and cultural values embodied in the national government," a government he anointed as the potential savior of America's destiny. Finally, Roosevelt attempted to embed the concept of conservation in the growing progressive impulse in cultural politics at the turn of the twentieth century. He not only situated conservation as a moral imperative, much like he had done by tying it to civil religion as previously mentioned, but he also connected it to the scientific wing of progressivism. By joining those polarizing positions in the singular notion of environmental protection, he worked to transcend the inherent divisions of progressivism.[23]

Rhetorical scholarship on Roosevelt's Governors' Conference speech has specifically identified the religious and moral dimensions of it. Daniel Buehler identified the president's turn to a jeremiad—a "political sermon"—to underscore the historical importance of conservation to the maintenance of cultural narratives such as the Frontier Myth and the American Dream. In doing that, President Roosevelt engaged America's past to demonstrate the "nation's reckless consumptive behaviors and its mismanagement of natural resources," and the need for his "radical conservation policy" as a remedy. Buehler concluded that Roosevelt's attempt to preserve the chaotic past undercut the acceptance of his "radical" policy and led to continued destructive practices of the environment. But Buehler also acknowledged that the speech "helped to usher in conservation and to improve the stewardship of natural resources."[24] Jessica Sheffield's work on the president's address to the Governors' Conference identified how he connected conservation to the duties a civilized and honorable citizenry needed to undertake, and related it to America's destiny to become a great nation if it could learn to use nature wisely. Sheffield concluded that the president's goal was to "recast conservation as a public (rather than private) and moral (rather than economic) issue."[25]

Both Buehler's and Sheffield's analyses focus on Roosevelt's speech as setting a moral foundation upon which to move his audiences to accept the idea of conservation—an idea they both surmised that Roosevelt saw as drastic. I disagree with that conclusion. In closely considering the multiple contexts and audiences involved with the discussion of environmental policy at the Governors' Conference, Roosevelt contextualized his conservation ideas as natural—not drastic—applications of political power. Furthermore, he avoided his typical discourse of moral indignation and made the conference resemble a forum for dispassionate discussion among varied elite constituencies with the singular goal of safeguarding the nation.

Roosevelt needed the Governors' Conference to affirm his institutional role as a fair-minded statesman and to prove that he was no rogue chief executive. For years prior to the event, the president took a holier-than-thou, belligerent attitude with those whom he believed stood against him. He waxed eloquently on the spiritual majesty of the environment and the need for conservation to ensure that divine state. He took great delight in denouncing corrupt and greedy sinners. He chose to go it alone and enact much of his environmental agenda without broad-based congressional support. He defiantly threatened to usurp state power with national oversight to force compliance with his will. He subjected congressmen to aggressive treatment, David Barry recounted as a journalist from that era, where the president would take a senator "by the buttonhole—by the whiskers . . . and talk to him" in "emphatic" tones.[26] By the time of the conference, even Roosevelt may have realized what his rhetorical maneuvering and bullying had cost him. According to Brinkley, Roosevelt had made enemies of a host of constituencies: corporate owners, preservationists, hunters, politicians, ranchers, prospectors, and even the western common folk who typically supported him.[27]

The president probably understood that if he had any chance to embed the notion of conservation in the nation's mind given his upcoming departure from the White House shortly after the Governors' Conference, he needed a new rhetorical strategy—one that lessened his image as a heavy-handed, singular entity who called for conserving the environment with appeals to moral uplift. During his near hourlong address in May 1908, he established himself as a pragmatic statesman, pushing aside his image as an imperious, morally righteous chief executive who demonized his critics. In addition he focused the media attention on detailing the production of the Governors' Conference, the dignified nature of his speech, and the scientific rhetoric of conference attendees rather than on its typical depiction of him as a fire-and-brimstone preacher obsessed with morality. Instead, this event heralded the economics of conservation for private interests, and set his plans to protect the environment as a natural—not radical—extension of American politics.

According to Timothy Egan, the president's crusade for conservation sought to "persuade people not just to cherish their natural heritage, but to understand that it was their right in a democracy to own it—every citizen holding a stake."[28] To foster that sense of cooperation, Roosevelt turned to what he knew best—myth.

Myths, sometimes dismissed as meaningless fairy tales, actually reflect a fundamental means for a group of individuals to cohere into a singular, national identity. "An American myth," Richard Hughes noted in *Myths America Lives By*, "is a story that conveys commonly shared convictions on the purposes and the meaning of the nation." Hughes observed that the most common myth of national origin involves America as a god-blessed chosen nation, comprised of undaunted heroes, destined to fulfill an exceptional existence. This storyline was most notably realized in the Puritans escape to the new world to find success and "freedom to place themselves under the absolute control of the law of God."[29] Myths popularize the values that affirm a nation's existence. Kenneth Burke likewise noted that these stories act as the "social tool for welding the sense of interrelationship" by which disparate groups of people "can work together for common social ends."[30]

Myths of national origin function at an unconscious level, in that they submerge the intricacies and ills of political ideologies and uncomfortable realities, transforming what remains into compelling units of social imagination. Roland Barthes referred to this phenomenon as the "depoliticized speech" of myth. "[Myth] abolishes the complexity of human acts," he identified, "it gives them the simplicity of essences, it does away with all dialectics . . . it organizes a world which is without contradictions because it is without depth." Mythic stories about the origin and development of a national culture, then, make the nation's actions "appear to mean something by themselves."[31] For Americans, the myths they told about their heroic fortitude and divine destiny led to policies that resulted in wholesale assaults against the environment for profits. Those policies appeared necessary because America had executed those policies; such logic in myths proved circular, indeed, but powerful nonetheless.

So Roosevelt needed to drastically revise the story about the country's past, in a way that would allow a reinterpretation of its present circumstances and its possible future. He needed to retell America's myth of origin so that it instead focused on conserving nature, not destroying it. To that end, he used his speech and the Governors' Conference to amend the story about the country's past. In the process of fundamentally revising America's foundational narrative of origin—the Frontier Myth—he focused on pioneers' inability to recognize the finite nature of the environment, and the problematic choices they had made as a result. In other words, his speech minimized the heroic nature of the nation's early settlers—they now appeared "average" and naïve, not extraordinary. His altered mythic narrative buoyed his agenda by offering new protagonists who exhibited the foresight to realize wise use of natural resources for future generations; such use would be determined by scientific thought and administered under federal government control. With many of the Governors' Conference attendees echoing these themes in their own presentations, and with the conference itself heralded in the media as the quintessential realization of presidential authority, Roosevelt opened a window into policy negotiations at just the right time—during a clear demonstration of his role as an institutional leader supported by friends and foes alike in a democratic effort to safeguard the country's future.

With his speech and the Governors' Conference, Roosevelt resembled a true statesman who appeared above the fray that he had engaged in years earlier. He essentially upended the Frontier Myth during his State of the Union-like address, re-conceptualized what it meant for America to be exceptional, and explained what he defined as a conservative approach to the conservation of the environment. To understand the intricacies of ideologies Roosevelt faced, his life and the choices he made with his discourse during his political career that led to the conference, as well as to appreciate the events of the conference itself as a rhetorical choice, this book will proceed as follows.

Chapter two focuses on the environmental intersection between America's life and Roosevelt's upbringing. From the first appearance of settlers in North America, the discourse surrounding nature identified it as something to be feared and thus conquered. Along with the seemingly unlimited expanses of natural bounty, pioneers used resources as if they were infinite. That behavior led to environmental consequences that threatened everyone. State and local governments attempted to set guidelines for natural resource use, but their ignorance of what constituted valid legislation—coupled with pressure from business interests to maintain their own unfettered access to nature—led to a contradictory jumble of laws and enforcement that made conservation almost impossible. With government unable to act effectively, cultural tensions erupted between preservationists who argued for the sanctity of the environment and conservationists, who dismissed that position and pushed instead for science-based policies regarding natural resources.

Into all of this Roosevelt grew up, with his personal debilitations that kept him homebound making him an avid reader about the outdoors. Through school and trips abroad, he learned of the attacks on the environment. With a burgeoning literary career and political prominence in his early years, he wrote about and spoke for wholesale changes to protect nature. Ascending to the White House, Roosevelt understood the complex rhetorical legacy surrounding the environment in the social imagination. He addressed that legacy in typical Roosevelt fashion: He became a sheriff rooting out villains; he embraced contradictory positions without much explanation, such as his support for preservationists who wanted the environment left untouched, conservationists who wanted nature used in ways to ensure its longevity, and nationalists who saw protection of the environment solely as the means to ensure American identity; and he became a mean-spirited critic of what he considered the legal and political shenanigans over who controlled nature.

Chapter three provides the philosophical underpinnings of Roosevelt's rhetorical performances in service to the environment. He believed that the chief executive had an unchallengeable mandate to do whatever was necessary to safeguard the nation. To that end, he engaged in an active management style, arbitrated morality, and reached out frequently to energize public constituencies and rally support for conservation. His principles of leadership foreshadowed the modern conception of what Tulis called the "rhetorical presidency." Political critics and everyday citizens alike, though, looked with trepidation at Roosevelt's rhetorical antics as he marched up and down the continent generating news about conservation and engaging in other activities considered unbecoming of the presidency.

To counter his growing image problem, to find a way to break through congressional blockades, and to check powerful business forces propping up legislator intransigence, Roosevelt employed his principles of leadership in the development of the Governors' Conference. First, he exploited the fledgling modern mass media by relating to it in ways contemporary presidents would not dare. He became a good friend to journalists, wrote copy for them, and allowed them the favors of being located in the White House. He also became a scourge to those he believed violated his trust, barring them from any access to political news. Second, he recognized how he could coopt a format for a speech event in a way that could counter his persona as a partisan bully. His speech, and the Governors' Conference, would resemble a modified version of a State of the Union event. Traditionally, the State of the Union had brought together members of Congress to read the president's message about a laundry list of issues facing the nation, a grand occasion that spoke to the institutional and respected position held by the president. Instead, Roosevelt planned to invite "everyone" to hear him speak on a singular topic related to the state of the union, utilizing the potential promise of that traditional event to renew his public image. Finally, the typical State of the Union speech, with its focus on collective identity, national values, historical origins, and the resulting policy recommendations, gave President Roosevelt the thematic choices to use in his speech as a platform to invoke again the nation's foundational narrative about its frontier origins. This time, however, he upended that story in a way that went far beyond what he had attempted to do previously.

Chapter four examines the speech itself, the foundations that Roosevelt had been laying for it since the beginning of his presidency, and how he pivoted from those positions to establish new themes for his Governors' Conference address. During the early years of his presidency, he engaged in public events that drew the media to report on his attempts to educate the public about wise use of the environment. Media outlets also gleefully reported his colorful castigations against business malefactors who threatened nature with their ravenousness. When he realized that he was not getting enough sustained and positive news coverage, or enough congressional support, he announced the Governors' Conference and, for seven months prior to the event, directed his administration to flood journalists with ready-made news copy heralding the unprecedented nature of collaboration that the conference foreshadowed. That news coverage established the majestic nature of this presidential event and prepared audiences for Roosevelt's speech.

With his speech, the president recalled America's mythic frontier origin. Instead of the pioneers representing symbols of American ingenuity, as they had been lauded in the Frontier Myth, he identified them as simply "average"—unlikely progenitors of the nation who lacked the basic common sense to realize what their actions were doing to the environment. But he absolved them of conscious wrongdoing, along with the business owners of his day. Instead, he blamed their behavior on a centuries-old trajectory of traditional thinking from which one group—the Founding Fathers—had freed themselves. Roosevelt's Frontier Myth now alleged that his own call for cooperation and conservatively prescribed use of natural resources echoed that of people like George Washington, who, according to Roosevelt, had created a similar conservation conference two centuries earlier. Because of that connection, Roosevelt's policies, and the conference itself, appeared to have the mythic endorsement of the Constitution's drafters, and the very real judicial consent by members of the Supreme Court in attendance at the conference. Finally, an examination of the other speeches during the conference—even those of his opponents—shows that they echoed Roosevelt's own speech about the need for conservation and the national government's supervisory role in it.

All told, Roosevelt's speech and the Governors' Conference generated near-universal support for his agenda, albeit with varying degrees of actual implementation and success, spanning several decades. He interpreted conservation as an economic and private business matter that could not work without the conservative and scientific management of the federal government to ensure the public good. His conservation event helped to catalyze most of the governors' support for a number of initiatives that they began immediately following the event, and it set the stage for others to continue the president's work through today. Orchestrated by the "father of conservation," this pivotal Governor's Conference, including Roosevelt's speech and the surrounding activities, clearly merits this book's sustained attention.

Two

The Environmental and Rhetorical Landscape

As a historian and a frontiersman, President Roosevelt probably understood that his conservation discourse competed against the immense weight of the social imagination regarding North America's development. For centuries citizens worshiped the notion of a God-blessed virgin land that belonged to them—an ownership that allowed them unfettered use (and misuse) of the land for survival, profit, and as a means to understand American identity. The interlocking and confusing rhetorical legacy surrounding the conquest, legislation, and cultural critique of the wilderness provided a complicated context that Roosevelt would eventually have to grapple with as he matured.

British settlers venturing to the North American continent in the early sixteenth century found a land of environmental bounty. Millions of acres of trees stretched beyond the horizon. Creatures of all types populated the land, sea, and sky. Fertile soil promised uncounted food supplies.[1] Ironically, the tremendous potential of these life-sustaining elements also brought with it overwhelming terror. Early settlers noted the physical dangers associated with the new environment. Journal entries and newspaper accounts routinely described the dangerous predators that settlers had to dodge each day, the threat of errant lightning strikes and resulting forest fires, and the hazard of trying to escape massive trees felled by fellow settlers. The majority of early pioneers obviously survived environmental attacks in the form of extreme weather and poisonous flora and fauna, but the regularity of such experiences perpetuated the perception of a grim existence in the new continent's wilderness.[2]

The term "wilderness" itself provided deep meaning to the settlers, not only about the physical stresses they faced, but the metaphysical ones as well. Roderick Nash observed that the term wilderness was "freighted with meaning" for early Americans. The word's origin associated it with chaos—with those natural elements over which humans had no control, both real and imagined.[3] Along with the actual beasts that posed threats, pioneers also believed they saw otherworldly, demonic creatures in the shadowy vastness of the forests.[4] In fact, the primeval harshness of the North American environment appeared evil. The Puritans, for example, called on the Old Testament as proof that the wilderness was a curse—a hellish place that regularly starved, dehydrated, diseased, and crippled those who lived in it.[5] North America appeared to be no new Eden to early settlers as they saw themselves suffering the same sentence as Adam and Eve did when that couple was cast into the wilderness.[6] To fulfill the theological promise of the New World as a site of sacred destiny, though, settlers would have to transform it into a paradise. In other words, the evils of the wilderness needed to be vanquished.[7]

CONQUERING THE ENVIRONMENT

Settlers' belief that the North America wilderness held the potential to become a paradise was a strategic one. "There is nothing natural about the concept of the wilderness," William Cronon noted, since "it is entirely a creation of the culture that holds it dear."[8] Early settlers constructed the meaning of the wilderness in ways to serve their goal of creating a physically safe utopia. That realization meant the removal of the continent's original inhabitants through both indirect and direct means. Europeans attempted to wish Native Americans away: the former's constant descriptions of the wilderness as untouched, Melanie Perreault observed, "figuratively emptied the land of its native inhabitants."[9] The prevalent stereotype of Native Americans as curious creatures, savages, and lawbreakers likewise minimized their human presence in the wilderness.[10] Their symbolic dismissal, however, was accompanied by more extreme measures that impacted the natural environment.

Beyond the military assaults, biological warfare, and displacement to reservations that occurred over time, Native Americans faced a fundamental threat to their food supply.[11] For centuries the Plains Indians had relied on the buffalo as both sustenance and a focal point of their culture. While they did hunt the great beasts, they lived by the creed, "Don't kill more meat than you think you can skin and your horse can pack home." They appeared to be no catastrophic menace to the longevity of this particular animal.[12] But with the Spanish's introduction of the horse to the hunt, the creation of the six-shooter, and the eventual mid-nineteenth-century governmental policy to deal with all Native Americans once and for all, the buffalo became a target for slaughter. "Buffalo war parties went west by train," Carolyn Merchant outlined, "shooting buffalo from train windows. . . . Records showed 120 buffalo killed in 40 minutes and 2,000 in a month. The average buffalo hunter killed one hundred a day. One hundred thousand buffalo were killed each year until they were on the verge of extinction, removing the subsistence base from Indian cultures."[13] The assault on this animal served as an attempt to starve and to remove Native Americans from the supposed uninhabited wilderness to make way for an imagined paradise. But this act also demonstrated the settlers' cultural shift from exorcising environmental evil as a means of survival to conquering it as a profit-making venture.

The common notion that Puritans came to the New World seeking religious freedom overshadowed the practical reality that they embraced. John Winthrop, delivering the sermon, "A Model of Christian Charity," aboard the *Arbella* before landing at the Massachusetts Bay Colony in the seventeenth century, spoke as meaningfully about financial success as he opined about sacred obligation.[14] In fact, his opening statement set the grounds for life in North America: "GOD ALMIGHTY in his most holy and wise providence, hath soe disposed of the condition of mankind, as in all times some must be rich, some poore, some high and eminent in power and dignity; others mean and in submission."[15] Thus, settlers eventually viewed the dangers of the wilderness as a means to a free-market end in which wealth and power could be extracted from its resources, such as through the sale of buffalo meat and hides. Unlike Native Americans, who typically used nature just to survive, settlers sought to profit from conquering the wilderness.[16]

The slaughter of buffaloes echoed the attacks on many species. For example, after Europe hunted its beaver population to extinction, it turned its attention to North America with the development of markets for fur trading in the seventeenth century. The overhunting of beavers by settlers in the new wilderness created steep declines in that animal population. What pioneers initially failed to recognize was the impact the near-disappearance of beavers had on the environment. Beavers' dam-building behavior provided a necessary link in the ecological chain: without their dams to create water pockets and habitats for numerous other animals, such as frogs, fish, and birds, those animal populations decreased as well.[17] While birds had been hunted for centuries, the advent of mass publications in the eighteenth century popularizing bird plumage as adornments exacerbated the need to hunt them vigorously. More hunters, more millinery trade, and more shopping districts in America had led to the destruction of more than five million birds by the late nineteenth century; many species were exterminated, including the passenger pigeon, great auk, yellow-winged green parrot, and the Labrador duck.[18] Like the near-extermination of beavers, the diminishing of bird populations—whether to provide feathers or food—meant the decrease of that species' ability to control insect populations, insects that proved destructive to farmers' crops.[19]

Another natural resource that seventeenth-century colonists attacked was the forests. Psychologically speaking, removing the forests reflected the early settlers' fear of those shadowy and frightening domains. Practically speaking, removing the forest led to profit. Tobacco production flourished in North America, generating huge revenues, once loggers cut away trees on the fertile land needed for growing that plant. With funding from Great Britain, the timber market between continents emerged.[20] Loggers cut trees for ship building, bridge construction, and firewood. The problem with cutting trees stemmed from loggers' attitude about timber acquisition: they maintained a "cut-and-run" policy, believing that timber, like other resources, were inexhaustible. As trees in the eastern portion of North America diminished, lumbermen moved west. Cheap labor, along with modern technology such as the circular saw and the steam-powered sawmill in the early 1800s, allowed timber barons to cut devastating swaths across most of what would become the United States, laying waste to trees thousands of years old.[21] Moreover, the introduction of the locomotive to the timber industry decades later—machines that belched fire to transport lumber across the country—made forest fires a more common occurrence, ironically destroying areas that loggers would target.[22] With so many trees cut by as early as the 1700s, the climate had begun changing. Fewer trees meant drier air and land conditions, fostering elemental deviations that included more hurricanes, soil erosion, dirt-clogged waterways, and the further diminishment of forest animal populations.[23]

Settlers looked not just to the sky for resources, nor to what they saw on the land itself. They also sought wealth below ground. By the mid-nineteenth century, America had become the "greatest mining nation in the world."[24] The California gold rush contributed greatly to that national title. Like the loggers, miners were mobile as scores of them quickly abandoned one potential site for another, bringing with them their hydraulic mining and chemical extraction processes. Hydraulic mining allowed workers to push hundreds of gallons of water through tubes at high speed to separate gold from tons of gravel. To complete the process, workers used a cyanide and/

or mercury solution to aid in the gold extraction process; the runoff from the former and the toxic waste from the latter polluted water systems and poisoned untold numbers of animals and fish.[25]

The settlers' notion of a chaotic wilderness needing to be tamed, their compact with God to thrive materially, and the centuries-old belief that North American environmental resources were infinite led to what appeared to be an all-out assault on nature. This attack, though, did not go unnoticed by local, state, and national legislators. Unfortunately, many laws passed to moderate use of the environment tended to aggravate the problem.

LEGISLATING THE ENVIRONMENT

Land represented one of the most regulated resources. In simple terms, the purpose of land involved putting it to use, not only to reduce the evil lurking in darkened forests, but also to create an idealized civilization of interconnected farmsteads populated by spiritually fulfilled people.[26] Ironically, others sought to use the land in ways that ran contrary to the idyllic notion of modest homesteader communities.

Congress saw agricultural development of the North American territory as the means to cement the new nation's status as a world power. Since it did not have the power to tax citizens directly in the nation's early days, it needed to raise money through the sale of land to new settlers.[27] Congress passed the 1785 Land Ordinance, which called on government surveyors to determine rectangular settlement plots measuring 640 acres. These plots demarcated potential townships across the country and earmarked land to be sold to settlers at auction for one dollar per acre. Over the next twenty years, Congress introduced several variations in that law. For instance, it raised minimum prices, established minimum land purchases, and authorized a credit payment system for buyers. Since some price increases were beyond most farmers' means, and they were supposed to be the most important beneficiaries of public land policy, Congress passed the "Log Cabin Law" in 1841. It allowed a male or female head (widow) of the household to claim 160 acres of surveyed land by "squatting" on it, building a house, and working the land as a farmer or rancher, paying no more than $1.25 per acre when the land came to auction.[28] A series of laws passed in the latter part of the nineteenth century appeared to aid farmers' acquisition of land: The Homestead Act of 1862 gave anyone who improved 160 acres in the Great Plains area, and who remained for five years, complete ownership of that land; the Timber Culture Act of 1873 likewise gave title to 160 acres if that person improved at least forty acres by planting trees; and the 1877 Desert Land Act provided ownership of 640 acres at $1.25 an acre if the settler irrigated the land within three years.[29]

Rather than provide an organized system of land development for single-family farmers, laws—along with questionable relationships between speculators, businesses, and government officials—created an illogical and corrupt system that privileged those individuals and companies that appeared largely indifferent to the development of the environment. In other words, the laws tended to favor those concerned only with generating profit at the expense of others who actually wanted to work the land. For example, the Yazoo land fraud, perpetrated by members in the Georgia legislature in 1795, authorized the sale of thirty-five million acres in Mississippi and Alabama to four companies for about a penny an acre; some Georgia legislators were affiliated with those companies and planned to sell the land at exorbitant prices.[30]

Many of the laws that set land purchases for farmers at 160 acres, such as the Homestead Act, were based on erroneous information: rainfall amounts in the West called for settlers to have much larger acreages to farm effectively. Even with the later Desert Land Act that upped parcels to 640 acres, the additional requirement for irrigating that land was beyond the knowledge and capability of most individual farmers (only a third were successful by 1888).[31] Furthermore, the Homestead Act, seen as the solution to give easterners a labor outlet by going west and developing the territory, largely failed. Unemployed easterners and their families did not have the funds to travel, let alone survive while waiting for their crops to grow and be taken to market.[32]

Greed and corruption, more so than incompetence, seemed to create the most problems. Corporate ranchers gobbled up the free land to drive cattle once the Plains Indians had been exiled from it. Ranchers saw cattle as wealth, not food, and ensured that they had the acreage to maintain their herds by using barbed wire to keep other settlers at bay. With cattle concentrated in grassland areas, they overfed and exposed the soil to erosion.[33] In other parts of the country, jockeying between wealthy businessmen and politicians had led to acreage price increases that prevented poor farmers from acquiring land. Most laws failed to differentiate between a potential homeowner and an agent working for a company.[34] Thus, businessmen took advantage of laws such as the Timber Culture Act to purchase millions of acres for logging. In fact, politicians of this era "even managed to get through a law that exonerated all against whom criminal suits had been brought for stealing federal timber."[35]

One of the most egregious land frauds, but in hindsight quite humorous, involved several Swamp Land Acts passed during the mid-1800s. These laws gave Congress the power to give "swampy and overflowed federal lands" to states, reflecting the federal notion that states would need to make the land usable. Since the laws governing the determination of what constituted swampland were, in the words of historian William Wyant, "poorly drawn," state agents administered the laws in criminal ways. For example, some states claimed that valuable forest areas were in fact swampland, even though this land had been surveyed to be in "high and dry areas." Wyant recalled the legend of a Mississippi state agent who "was said to have chosen as swamp all tracts over which a boat could pass. He hitched a canoe to a work animal and dragged the canoe over good pine country," thereby designating that land as swampy. Although state governments proved to be "terrible" land managers, probably due to the undue pressure companies could put upon local and state politicians, the federal government appeared almost as bad.[36]

Perhaps the greatest abuser of public land policy and co-conspirator with the national government was the railroad industry. In the mid-nineteenth century, Congress offered public land to private railroad companies well before settlers had a chance to claim millions of acres of free land, sometimes enticing those companies with federal grants that contained a "stench of corruption."[37] The infamous Union Pacific/Crédit Mobilier railroad scandal involved congressional representatives providing millions of dollars in grants to Union Pacific. Union Pacific then paid the construction company it secretly owned—Crédit Mobilier—to build the first transcontinental railroad; given their seeming independence, the latter could overcharge for construction costs without responsibility laid at the feet of the former. Crédit Mobilier then bought stocks in Union Pacific at much reduced prices and gave some of those shares to several Congressmen, who could then sell those stocks on the open market for handsome profits. That bribe to legislators initially blocked an investigation into the relationship between Union Pacific and Crédit Mobilier. In 1872 the fraud was exposed, leading the government to refrain from giving large land grants to railroad companies.[38]

When the federal government did hold legitimate land auctions, Wyant concluded: "[C]apitalists tried to buy up choice parcels before the settlers got to them. Local people, jealous of outsiders, conspired openly to keep the government from getting fair market value. . . . Sometimes they organized 'claims clubs' with which they shook down or terrorized outsiders who came in to compete with men already on the scene. . . . Against these forces large and small, the central authority was weak. Federal officers not infrequently gave up and joined in the plunder."[39] Railroads clearly needed to crisscross the continent to provide pathways for national development, but in the process, the unscrupulous deal-making between government and railroad interests abetted other industries' unscrupulous desires to reach and to exploit the resources of forests, mountains, and animal habitats.[40]

The human corruption and attending ravages of the environment spurred several cultural responses. For some, nature needed to be safeguarded for its own sake (preservationists). For others, the environment needed protecting so that it could be used efficiently (conservationists). And still other advocates called for nature's defense because of its relevance to the symbolic and practical embodiment of American identity (nationalists).

CULTURAL RESPONSES TO ENVIRONMENTAL ABUSE

Although the first settlers considered the North American wilderness a devilish and foreboding environment, that attitude slowly changed. Some early American thinkers—the Transcendentalists—took a more philosophical stance about nature, pushing back against the idea of casting the environment as simply a collection of raw materials in a hellish landscape.[41] Ralph Waldo Emerson's famed 1836 essay, "Nature," called for readers to consider a different relationship with the environment, one that recognized the need to be in harmony with it—not its antagonist—so as to receive its profound truths. "Nature satisfies the soul purely by its loveliness," Emerson wrote, "and without any mixture of corporeal benefit. I have seen the spectacle of morning from the hill-top over against my house, from day-break to sun-rise, with emotions which an angel might share."[42] Emerson's protégé, Henry David Thoreau, likewise published a stirring account of his self-imposed, solitary exile into the wilds of New England in 1854. His sojourn, recounted in *Walden*, described his immersion in nature so that he could receive transcendent insights about humanity's relationship with the divine.[43]

Borrowing from the eighteenth-century work of Edmund Burke, Transcendentalists wrote about the "sublime" nature of the wilderness. Natural vistas reflected a supernatural, majestic, near-infinite, and unmatched beauty that evoked deep passions. These unparalleled scenes—mountainous regions that touched the sky, rolling hills of lush vegetation, and unchecked rivers that ended in breathtaking waterfalls—seemed akin to holy places where visitors could experience communion with God.[44] As Merchant noted,

"Revering wilderness as bespeaking God rather than denigrating it as evil, as had their Puritan ancestors, many transcendentalists came to feel it should be cherished and preserved."[45]

Artists in the mid-nineteenth century visually celebrated nature as a sublime manifestation of God's bounty. Thomas Cole, founder of the Hudson River School (considered the first school of American art), and other painters "represented an America of rolling hills, pristine lakes, and dense forests, of occasional farms and villages surrounded by a vast, Edenic . . . wilderness."[46] These ethereally beautiful, painted scenes that became hugely popular argued that nature should be left unsullied by human exploitation. By preserving nature, Americans stayed connected to God and embodied a national character unmatched by foreign peoples. The intent of this "landscape art," John Opie noted, "was to root nationalism in the physical reality of the republic—purple mountains majesty, amber waves of grain, the fruited plane. . . . [W]ilderness stood as a desirable, even utopian state, not a hostile forest to be cleared and planted as quickly as possible in domestic crops."[47]

Preservationists were not alone in calling for the protection of the environment—conservationist thinkers did too. However, conservationists largely rejected the notion that wild areas represented sacred spaces for humans to use for spiritual development. They argued for protection so that the wilderness could continue to provide resources for successive generations.

Conservationist thinking burst into the public consciousness in the latter part of the nineteenth century. Credited as the first conservationist, diplomat and philologist George Marsh published a well-received account of humanity's impact on the natural world.[48] *Man and Nature* offered dire warnings about the ramifications of the continued assault on the environment, particularly the stripping of forests from the continent. "When the forest is gone," he warned in 1864, along with its ability to store moisture, "the land would grow dry and strangle the waterways with debris." He granted that everything in the natural world—animals, insects, fish—all preyed on one another, but that they did so in a balanced way; humans, on the other hand, hunted their "victims with reckless destructiveness." According to Marsh, that inability to respect balance would lead to humanity's downfall: "The earth is fast becoming an unfit home for its noblest inhabitant, and another era of equal human crime and human improvidence . . . would reduce it to such a condition of impoverished productiveness, of shattered surface, of climatic excess, as to threaten the depravation, barbarism, and perhaps even extinction of the species."[49]

Marsh's book made a life-changing impact on someone who would become pivotal to the conservationist movement in the Roosevelt administration—Gifford Pinchot. Pinchot's parents gave him a copy of Marsh's book in 1886 on his twenty-first birthday and, along with their interest in Marsh's work, convinced their son to take up a career in forestry. At that point in time, there existed no forestry profession in the United States, so Pinchot traveled to France and enrolled in that country's forestry service and learned about the scientific administration of nature. After returning to the United States, Pinchot became a forest agent for the Department of Interior, and by 1898, was named as head of the Forestry Division in the Department of Agriculture.[50] Pinchot operated the division on what he called "exceedingly simple principles," which included recognizing that conservation meant development of natural resources for use, minimizing waste in acquiring resources, and recognizing that the public good must be served instead of private interests.[51] For him, efficiency in managing commercial use, not spiritual awakening, proved the most important element for protecting the environment.

The conservationists wanted to preserve the land for use economically. The nationalists, on the other hand, argued for protecting the environment because it represented the catalyst for American identity. One such proponent was Frederick Jackson Turner. As a young historian, Turner broke rank with senior scholars when he presented his "frontier thesis" at the 1893 American Historical Association conference. In "The Significance of the Frontier in American History," he alleged that American identity came from something more than "germs" transplanted from European lands. For him, the continuous movement west and the brutal experiences that settlers faced had transformed them into something exceptional.[52] He wrote:

> "[To] the frontier the American intellect owes its striking characteristics. That coarseness and strength combined with acuteness and inquisitiveness; that practical, inventive turn of mind, quick to find expedients; that masterful grasp of material things, lacking in the artistic but powerful to effect great ends; that restless, nervous energy; that dominant individualism, working for good and for evil, and withal that buoyancy and exuberance which comes with freedom—these are traits of the frontier, or traits called out elsewhere because of the existence of the frontier."

The problem, as Turner saw it, was the fact that the 1890 federal census had officially declared the frontier closed.[53] That meant American civilization—as an identity of pioneering and iron-willed people renewing their life-force in the frontier crucible—could not sustain itself if the remaining wild environment was destroyed.The nationalist idea of a frontier-inspired culture, along with the intellectual positions of preservationists and conservationists, converged in the development of Yellowstone National Park, established during the Ulysses S. Grant administration in 1872. Congress and President Grant set aside more than two million acres in Wyoming for the first national park.[54] It seemed to be the response to a number of concerns related to environmental protection.[55] By the late nineteenth century, medical and political advocates warned that the effects of city life—constant bombardment of information, enervating work experiences in offices and factories, and overemphasis on consumer culture—had increased the level of nervousness in people and created a widespread state of depression and moral malaise.[56] Yellowstone acted as a wild playground for tourists and campers to hearken back to a simpler time and harmonize with nature—both aesthetically and physically—to rebuild their psyche.

Furthermore, the designation of Yellowstone as a park signaled a shift in national policy. Whereas previous programs transferred large areas of the public domain into small plots of land privately owned, Yellowstone demonstrated that the federal government was more actively concerned with the management of public land. For example, its oversight of Yellowstone spurred it to send the US Army to the park to stop hunters from slaughtering animals, prevent loggers from cutting down trees haphazardly, and generally to maintain the pristine nature of the area.[57] It seemed as if Yellowstone appealed to preservationists who wanted the beauty of nature untouched, the conservationists who wanted the environment used responsibly, and those nationalists who looked to continue enjoying the frontier experience.

However, Yellowstone reflected and exacerbated a number of issues detrimental to the environment and American culture. It became a site of "acrimonious debate" for years between preservationists and those conservationists who wanted more use of it—particularly those subsistence settlers who lived near it and had been using it to hunt and fish for food, and to build their log cabin homes.[58] With the arrival of the military to police the area, homesteaders' actions once associated with the pioneering lifestyle had become federal offenses labeled as poaching and trespassing. In fact, park officials argued against the pioneer/nationalist lifestyle, blaming it for animal population decreases and wildfires within the park boundaries.[59] The military also appeared helpless to stop the incursions into Yellowstone by frontiersmen. Hunters and loggers were intimately familiar with the hidden trails throughout the park (some even lived in the park), while the soldiers were not. Soldiers even accepted bribes to help hunters acquire targets in the park, or drove animals outside Yellowstone's boundaries to make the killing legal. Moreover, the military's official attempt to manage wildlife in the park also proved counterproductive. To protect the elk population, soldiers hunted its predators regularly, but their efforts led to an explosion in the number of elk. As a result, the elk overgrazed, leading to soil erosion and a decline in the trees that beavers preferred to build dams; without the dams "ecologically rich wetlands" diminished.[60] Finally, the army's supervision of Yellowstone coincided with renewed efforts to remove Native Americans from the wilderness. Several tribes in the area ceded their claim to land based on an 1868 treaty that assured them they would be granted hunting rights within the park. The federal government rejected the tenets of the treaty and banned Native Americans from entering Yellowstone as they supposedly posed a threat to park visitors.[61]

Yellowstone provided no clear, uncontested symbol for any ideological group. The military failed to stop the profligate attacks on animal life and trees that both conservationists and preservationists abhorred. Park officials attacked the meaning of national identity when they castigated and outlawed behaviors that had supposedly transformed European settlers into Americans. The park also represented a passive tourist site, not a location for a rough-and-tumble frontier experience that nationalists desired. Some politicians deemed the financial upkeep of the park as an unnecessary expenditure.[62] The most obvious problem stemmed from local policy-making that failed to understand the complexity of environmental management, such as the directive to have soldiers cull animal populations, which resulted in severe consequences to the park's ecological system.[63] The struggle between competing ideologies at a political, economic, and cultural level did not reflect a coherent national consciousness about the need to consider natural resources more thoughtfully.[64]

Advocates supporting whatever side needed a singular and powerful voice to transform disparate positions into a unified movement to protect the environment. Theodore Roosevelt would represent that voice, a voice impassioned by his learned knowledge of the environment and its history, as well as the direct experiences he had in countless wildernesses.

ROOSEVELT: THE EARLY YEARS

Roosevelt's legacy on environmental protection began with the consequences surrounding his birth in 1858. As noted in his autobiography, he was a "sickly, delicate boy," and as a result, his parents largely confined him to the house for his early years. His enjoyment derived from reading and, given his inability to spend large amounts of time outside, he developed a keen interest in reading about nature. Thus, when he was allowed outside, he spent his time learning firsthand about the denizens of the environmental world. He recounted passing an outdoor market that displayed a "dead seal laid out on a slab of wood. That seal filled me with every possible feeling of romance and adventure." Each day he passed it he took notes on its dimensions and began to write his own natural history about it. With the seal's skull, along with small animals he kept, both living and dead, the teenage Roosevelt transformed a part of his parent's house into what he euphemistically labeled the "Roosevelt Museum of Natural History." In fact, over the years Roosevelt would compile such a collection of samples, and generate so many personal and detailed observations of nature, that he eventually donated his collection to the Smithsonian and to the Museum of Natural History in New York.[65]

As he grew to young adulthood, Roosevelt recognized the environment as an arena for him to develop his once-frail frame, and as a site of intellectual pursuit. He hunted, hiked, climbed, and rode horses in the northeastern United States, building his body to allow him to traverse greater areas.[66] He read voraciously about animals of all kinds, particularly birds, and traveled with his parents several times to Europe, where, Douglas Brinkley wrote, Roosevelt "observed nature like a budding biologist."[67] Roosevelt planned to use his college years to study natural science at Harvard, taking several related courses and presenting his research at natural history clubs. Yet, he lost interest in pursuing science at Harvard given his dissatisfaction with the way the university provided natural history education, and due to his pride being stung that his teachers never encouraged him to pursue his ambitions.[68]

Roosevelt's marriage, and election to the New York State Assembly in the early 1880s, did not mean he was finished with his passion for wilderness. He took a memorable trip to the Dakota Badlands in 1883 where he experienced the majesty and the tragedy of that wilderness area. He wrote in his autobiography of a "land of vast silent spaces, of lonely rivers," and of trackless plains that "shimmered and wavered in the heat."[69] Publishing his account of that trip in the 1885 *Hunting Trips of a Ranchman*, Roosevelt reveled in the opportunity to embrace nature as a rancher and a hunter. Despite being a hunter himself, Roosevelt had, from childhood, been concerned with the welfare of animals. He looked unkindly on those who brutally mistreated them.[70] He hunted for game, and for the occasional trophy as demonstration of his masculinity, but not to exhaust a species.[71] In his book he railed against those responsible for the plight of the buffalo: "Their destruction has gone on with appalling rapidity and thoroughness; and the main factors in bringing it about have been the railroads, which carried hordes of hunters into the land and gave them means to transport their spoils to market. . . . The extermination of the buffalo has been a veritable tragedy of the animal world."[72]

When Roosevelt's wife and mother died within hours of one another in February 1884, he retreated immediately to the Badlands again for a time. Over the next few years he returned repeatedly to the area and experienced firsthand the effects of environmental abuse. Roosevelt looked on helplessly as his North Dakota ranch was buried and his cattle destroyed in an 1887 blizzard. Come the fall, the "region's prairie grass," Ted Steinberg noted, "had lost the battle with ranchers, ever eager to stock the range with more animals than it could reasonably bear." For Roosevelt, the "Badlands must have offered a melancholy sight" with wide expanses stripped of vegetation and game.[73] Two years later, that spurred him to organize with like-minded thinkers and form the Boone and Crockett Club, an organization dedicated to the protection of wildlife, particularly game animals.[74] A proper environment of plentiful flora and fauna fit within Roosevelt's notion of the wilderness as a proving ground for Americans.

During the 1890s, Roosevelt's responsibilities on the New York Board of Police Commissioners and as the assistant secretary of the Navy involved matters other than the environment. But he continued promoting the protection and the use of nature.

In 1893, Roosevelt edited a collection of essays related to hunting and conservation, in turn becoming the publisher of the work via his Boone and Crockett Club.[75] Roosevelt's own book, *The Wilderness Hunter,* also appeared in bookstores that same year. Readers undoubtedly recognized the glee with which he wrote of a hunter's experiences—the "free, self-reliant, adventurous life . . . the wild surroundings, the grand beauty of the scenery, the chance to study the ways and habits of the woodland creatures,"—all of which cultivated that "vigorous manliness" necessary for national advancement. In these accounts of the majestic vistas, he sounded like a preservationist. Other anecdotes reflected his conservationist and nationalist leanings. His book described the daily routine of a hunter and rancher in picturesque terms, devoting each chapter to a game animal. In hunting moose, for example, he noted with awe the "vast pine and birch forests of the Northeast," and the "stupendous mountain masses of the Rockies." Despite the focus on hunting, Roosevelt repeatedly reminded his readers that true hunting was not about commercialism, but about survival and trophy, as both limited the amount of damage done to animal populations. "Killing a deer from a boat while the poor animal is swimming," he declared, "or on snowshoes as it flounders helplessly in the deep drifts, can only be justified on the plea of hunger. . . . Whoever indulges in any of these methods, save from necessity, is a butcher pure and simple, and has no business in the company of true sportsmen."[76]

When he attained the New York governorship in November 1898, Roosevelt immediately went to work pushing an environmental agenda. His first Annual Message as Governor in 1899 contained a brief, almost perfunctory statement regarding the importance of the state's forests, along with the need to enforce fish and game protection laws.[77] Coincidentally, though, the new governor had in the same year become good friends with someone also interested in nature's welfare—Gifford Pinchot. The two men worked together during Roosevelt's tenure to reorganize the Fisheries, Game, and Forest Commission to act more efficiently in its tasks. Over the course of his two-year tenure as governor, Roosevelt sponsored the creation of Palisades Park to halt mining in a 700-acre area between New York and New Jersey, and pushed for changes in school curricula to include subjects such as geography and natural history to spur interest in the environment. His second Annual Message in 1900, which Brinkley labeled the "most important speech about conservation ever delivered by a serious American politician up until that time," catalogued a list of problems facing New York's natural resources: lack of pioneer-like game wardens, railroad encroachment, indiscriminate killing of birds, and floods and droughts that stemmed from forest destruction.[78]

The emergence of the environment as a national issue, however, required two fateful deaths. President William McKinley's vice-president died, resulting in Roosevelt's elevation to that position during his second and last year as governor. The other death involved the assassination of McKinley in 1901. Vice President Roosevelt knew McKinley had been shot but thought he would recover, so he decided to go camping in the Adirondacks to "reassure the American people that the national crisis was over." Mythic in its own right, Roosevelt learned of the president's death as he sat atop a mountain surveying a breathtaking natural environment.[79]

ROOSEVELT: THE PRESIDENTIAL YEARS

The initial announcement of Roosevelt's presidency generated well wishes for the most part, but not everyone greeted the news with celebration.[80] Mark Hanna, Republican senator and party boss, famously bemoaned, "Now look, that damned cowboy is President of the United States." Hanna, who had had a successful career in the coal industry before Congress, and who had been instrumental in blocking anti-trust legislation as a senator, must have feared what the cowboy popularly represented—an impulsive and solitary figure that never backed down from a fight.[81] And as Roosevelt himself wrote about his own adventures in the Dakota territory, he considered the cowboy a "bold, free spirit" who longs for "where the prairies stretch out into billowy plains of waving grass, girt only by the blue horizon . . . where the glory and the burning splendor of the sunsets kindle the blue vault of heaven and the level brown earth."[82] On the one hand, a cowboy as president could bode well for cattle ranchers since the former was typically in the employ of the latter.[83] On the other hand, a cowboy president could pose a threat to business interests that menaced his cherished environment. As Brinkley noted, Hanna's worst fears were realized when Roosevelt turned out to be a "pro-forest, pro-buffalo, cougar-infatuated, socialistic land conservationist."[84]

Roosevelt's interest in nature and his elevation to the presidency coincided with a growing political movement many may have considered socialistic: progressivism. By the turn of the twentieth century, large segments of the population had begun rebelling against mounting problems that appeared to foster inequality and that affected the nation's wellbeing. Wage workers seemed to have no voice in how long they could work, in what sorts of conditions, or even their choice of work given the power of corporate owners to direct their own fortunes at the expense of others. The burgeoning consumer leisure culture, in the form of saloons and movie houses, seemed to threaten the moral center of the nation. Corruption at governmental levels reached all-time highs. Race and ethnic issues, particularly in growing numbers of urban areas, seemed ready to tear the country apart.[85] These roiling and disruptive cultural issues called forth reformers—progressives—who championed government action to punish wrongdoers and provide equal opportunities for workers and owners to become financially successful. They also promoted both Christian and science-based theories as remedies for America's problems, and they called for community organizations to help individuals experience political, economic, and social freedom.[86]

Some progressives turned their attention specifically to environmental issues. Michael McGerr noted that at the turn of the twentieth century, "a growing number of people questioned the uncontrolled exploitation of natural resources," and believed that by "preventing the wealthy from monopolizing resources, conservation would ensure opportunity and equality for succeeding generations." These progressives identified fresh air, forests, parks, and unspoiled scenery as a cure for urban citizens suffering the enervating effects of an increasingly industrialized modern life. Beyond these urban matters, some reformers worried that the romanticized view of rural life—the yeoman farmer as the bedrock of American life—suffered as well since increasing numbers of people fled farming areas to live in cities. The Country Life Movement, ironically comprised of middle-class urban activists and academics, urged farmers to cooperate with one another instead of holding to the mythic notion of rugged individualism. That push for cooperation undergirded the progressive idea that various constituencies needed to be brought together by experts so as to safeguard the nation's future.[87]

Roosevelt's own progressive leanings, and the power of the presidency, gave him what he believed to be the license to curb the destruction of natural resources and to try and make the lives of all citizens that much better.[88] The President's First Annual Message alerted the country to his thinking about environmental issues. Written to Congress in December 1901, he noted that places such as Yellowstone fostered increases in animal populations and, if properly supervised, prevented those animals from overgrazing, loosening too much soil, and causing flooding. It was paramount that forest reserves remain intact as sanctuaries, he argued, not only for animals but also for the "use and benefit of our people as a whole" to "find rest, health, and recreation." Forested areas would not go untouched; rather, with proper management, they would be used to sustain their existence into the future and continue to contribute "their share to the welfare of the people." He acknowledged that forests constituted "natural reservoirs" but that government was needed to assist in water management in order to reclaim arid land. For the topic of reclamation and irrigation, he proposed that the "object of the government is to dispose of the land to settlers who will build homes upon it," which meant that "water must be brought within their reach." He reiterated the idea of the public welfare, in that any reclamation project must serve the "people as a whole" and not simply "satisfy selfish personal or local interests."[89]

Although Roosevelt's thoughts on the environment represented just a brief part of the annual message, the progressive tenor of it was clear: government actions needed to be taken to protect nature for everyone's benefit, even while using it now so that it remained available for the next generation. That tone, coupled with his "cowboy" traits, led him to act in ways that seemed aggressive in both his personal and his political life.

For example, President Roosevelt loved animals. He allowed his children to turn the White House into a menagerie in the same way he had done in his parents' house. Beyond several dogs, his children owned an assortment of animals including a rabbit, pony, bear, pig, rooster, lizard, and snakes.[90] Of particular interest to Roosevelt, though, were birds. During visits by legislators and other important guests to the White House, Roosevelt would rush them to a window to watch some specimen. To protect birds from plume hunters, he acted in that cowboy way—impetuously. When he learned that ornithologists wanted to make Pelican Island off the coast of Florida into a federally protected bird refuge, and that there was no law stopping him, he famously intoned, "I so declare it." After this executive order, and to safeguard those birds further, he called for vigorous prosecution and imprisonment of poachers found at the refuge.[91] Other bird sanctuaries would follow and, by the end of his presidency, Paul Cutright wrote, Roosevelt had "accomplished more for the protection of wildlife . . . than all the twenty-four Presidents who had preceded him."[92]

The president found his credentials as an animal lover burnished, ironically, on his first hunting trip as president. In 1902 the president decided to visit Mississippi during bear hunting season. After several days he was frustrated that he and his party had not seen any prey. Near the end of the trip, the party's leader captured a small black bear, tied it to a tree, and summoned Roosevelt to shoot it. He refused. For him, the hunter represented a symbol of manliness and honor—the embodiment of frontier mythos—and killing a helpless animal ran counter to that idea. Roosevelt's refusal to shoot led the *Washington Post's* cartoonist to draw a cartoon that tickled the nation: it showed the president, holding his rifle with his right hand, his back turned to the captured bear, with his left arm stretched behind him and his left hand palm outward, signaling a stopping motion. The caption read, "Drawing the Line in Mississippi." That same cartoonist began adding a small bear to all his cartoons involving Roosevelt, which eventually got the attention of a toymaker, and the president's association with the teddy bear was born.[93]

Roosevelt's fierce appreciation of buffaloes and desire to protect them undoubtedly raised attention. He wanted the government to purchase all American buffalo from ranchers. Immediately after his reelection, he did just that. With another "proclamation" in June 1905, the president had earmarked more than sixty thousand acres of land in the Wichita Mountains to be used as a buffalo refuge.[94] This Rooseveltian decree appeared more personal and spoke to the president's ability to overlook race—during a time of rampant racism—when it involved safeguarding the environment.[95] He chose the Wichita Mountain area because of his admiration for Quanah Parker, a Comanche chief who attended his inauguration in March 1905. Having met the chief for the first time at that event, Roosevelt quickly developed a friendship with Parker, a man who shared his love of the buffalo.

Shortly after the inauguration, the president met Parker for a hunting trip in the Wichitas.[96] Unlike the stereotypical portrait of Native Americans-as-savages that was common for the era, the president demonstrated that concern for the environment signaled civilized thinking and that trumped prejudice.[97]

The triumph of the teddy bear and the significance of the Parker relationship notwithstanding, President Roosevelt's first forays into environmental management involved both protecting and preparing land for use. Embodying the mythos of the frontier cowboy, he safeguarded land by bringing the abusers of it to justice. Less than a year into his presidency, Roosevelt learned that several lumber and mining interests had been grabbing tracts meant for homesteaders in Oregon. He directed a special investigator to find out what they were doing and how they were doing it. The president learned that most members of that state's Congress and the Oregon Land Commissioner had colluded with companies to secure properties. Even though the prosecutions, convictions, and resignations of high-ranking officials for fraud and tampering with evidence lasted into Roosevelt's second term, and despite calls that his crusade negatively affected the state's Republican brand, the public appreciated his decisive handling of the affair.[98]

The president also looked with dismay at the vast amounts of arid land that could have been transformed with irrigation if the government had supported private industries in the construction of reservoirs decades before. Seizing on Roosevelt's statements about western irrigation in his first annual message, several Congressmen quickly drafted a bill calling for government funding in private reservoir construction. The president's energetic support led to the Reclamation Act becoming law less than six months later. By the time he left office, over three million acres had been successfully irrigated.[99]

Roosevelt's early and relatively quick success with land reclamation appeared easy in comparison to another project involving land and water—the Hetch Hetchy dam. That controversial project brought preservationists and conservationists in direct competition, with the president stuck right in the middle.[100]

Famed naturalist John Muir had lobbied Congress in the late nineteenth century to put Yosemite Valley under federal protection. When Yosemite National Park was established in 1890, it included the Hetch Hetchy Valley in California. Muir's push to save Yosemite stemmed from his love of trees, which had brought him into close contact and an eventual friendship with Gifford Pinchot at the time of the park's creation. And in another cosmic coincidence, Muir had accompanied Roosevelt during the president's 1903 trip through Yosemite, where Muir's extensive knowledge of the environment captivated Roosevelt and turned them both into mutual admirers.[101]

For the first few years of the twentieth century, San Francisco legislators made repeated calls to dam the Hetch Hetchy Valley, and each time they were denied. These salvos against the valley had involved Muir, Pinchot, and Roosevelt. Muir rallied public opinion around the aesthetic value of preserving Hetch Hetchy, while Pinchot affirmed the conservationist position that practical use for the greatest good superseded preserving natural beauty. The president tried to have it both ways. In a speech to the American Forest Congress in 1903, for example, he recognized that a forest's beauty was a "good in itself," but that that idea should be balanced with the need of clearing some forests for homesteaders.[102]

After the infamous earthquake and subsequent fires that ravaged San Francisco in April 1906, the city's legislators seized on the public's sympathy to call again for a dam that might have provided the water to minimize the fire damage. Muir wrote to Roosevelt in 1907, reminding him of their 1903 trip, the president's genuine awe of nature's majesty, and Roosevelt's appreciation of the preservationist's position. But he also warned Roosevelt that the American people would not stand for building a dam in the valley. The president was torn and sought alternate locations for a dam, but engineers reported that Hetch Hetchy was the only viable remedy. Roosevelt reluctantly sided with Pinchot in October 1907 (perhaps spurring Roosevelt to establish Muir Woods National Monument three months later), but Muir's public campaign over the next few years promoting preservationist thinking and deriding conservationism delayed the implementation of the reservoir's construction until well after Roosevelt left office.[103]

Perhaps more than anything else, Roosevelt wanted an orderly land management system to oversee the nation's resources. In 1903 he created the Public Land Commission to administrate the use and disposal of land regulated by the federal government. The commission offered several remedies to the legal muddle of laws that had long benefitted business interests over public ownership, including the issuing of permits for a limited time period—accompanied by a fee—for use of land. Companies involved with water power objected, calling for permits to be permanent and without cost.[104] The most strenuous objection may have come from the coal industry in the president's second term. Roosevelt called for coal land prices to be set at fair market value to stem the fraud perpetrated by speculators abusing loopholes to acquire that land. He proposed that coal lands be leased, not sold. Congress was slow to approve the leasing plan so Roosevelt wrote to the Senate and the House urging it to vote since "failure to prevent fraud . . . is peculiarly serious, because in so many cases the success of the fraudulent claimants means the prevention of the establishment of a home by some honest home seeker."[105] As Congress continued to resist the leasing plan, Roosevelt took action in another way: under the Coal Act of 1873, he claimed, he could direct the Department of the Interior to increase coal land prices to reflect their actual sales value since the act only set minimum prices, not maximum. A survey of coal land resulted in the monetary value having doubled since the 1873 act, and the land sold at much-increased prices.[106]

Roosevelt faced more opposition when he turned his attention to America's forests. However, he had a staunch ally in the form of Chief Forrester Pinchot. During the president's first term, Pinchot pushed for the nation's forest reserves to come under his control in the Department of Agriculture's Forest Service, transferring them from the General Land Office in the Department of the Interior. Both he and Roosevelt believed that governmental and scientific management of the forest reserves could extend their longevity. Both wanted more funding to train additional forestry agents to oversee timber protection. The opposition they faced to make this change was formidable: The Department of the Interior resisted the loss of its power; timber interests certainly lobbied not to change a system that it could abuse easily and regularly; and ranchers who had used forested lands for grazing rebelled since those lands, under Pinchot's control, would have usage fees attached.[107]

One of the most prominent obstacles to Federal government forest management was Senator William Clarke, dubbed one of the meanest and wealthiest men from Montana. Clarke and Roosevelt hated one another, as the former saw western land as the means to get rich while the latter saw it as a site for the physical and spiritual transformation of the citizenry. Working directly for John D. Rockefeller and Standard Oil, Clarke wanted to maintain the General Land Office's control over the transference of public land. According to Timothy Egan, it was the "perfect government agency . . . staffed by bureaucrats who neither knew nor cared for wild land in the West," and would be amenable to transferring land to Standard Oil so that it could create new rail lines from the Midwest to the East Coast. Clarke used his power in Congress to try and block any conservation legislation and employed the newspaper he owned to establish a steady drumbeat of opposition to the president's plans.[108]

To combat the resistance, Roosevelt believed that educating the populace about issues surrounding the forests was critical, so he took on that pedagogical role nearly every chance he could. Touring the western states in 1903, he stopped at Stanford University in California to discuss the sublime essence of trees. He took a preservationist stance when he declared that he "saw for the first time a grove of your trees, a grove which has taken the ages several thousands of years to build up. . . . There is nothing more practical . . . than the preservation of beauty." He condemned the timber industry that "skinned the land and was perfectly content for the sake of three years' profit . . . to leave a desert for the children of those who were to inherit the soil." He charged the audience to protect "these wonderful monuments of beauty." But Roosevelt made his conservationist intentions—the protection and use of the environment—known as well: "I am not advocating forest protection from the aesthetic standpoint only," he stated, "I do advocate the keeping of big trees, the great monarchs of the woods, for the sake of their beauty, but I advocate the preservation and wise use of the forests. . . . I am asking that the forests be used wisely for the sake of the successors of the pioneers."[109] Following Roosevelt's western states barnstorming and later speech events, along with his landslide victory for reelection in 1904, Congress finally agreed to transfer the forest reserves to Pinchot's control in early 1905.[110]

Roosevelt was not finished with protecting forested land and he continued to create enemies in the process. In 1907 an Agricultural Appropriations bill arrived on the president's desk for his signature. Because Congress disapproved of how Roosevelt and Pinchot prevented the timber industry from its unregulated use of that natural resource, the bill contained an amendment that prohibited the creation of any more forest reserves in several states. Members of Congress believed they had outfoxed Roosevelt; they assumed he would have no choice but to sign the bill or risk a denial of congressional-approved funds to the Department of Agriculture in the next year's budget cycle. Roosevelt and Pinchot plotted a countermove that would become known as Roosevelt's "midnight proclamations." The president planned to authorize twenty-one new forest reserves before he signed Congress's bill. He and Pinchot worked long hours over several days to write the proclamations that would turn sixteen million acres into National Forests. Once they were legally established, Roosevelt signed the Appropriations bill right before its deadline. Timber interests sued, claiming the Executive Branch had acted without the necessary congressional approval. The Supreme Court sided with Roosevelt, though, emboldening the cowboy-president to continue establishing monuments, refuges, and reserves.[111]

Roosevelt's desire to protect the nation's environmental resources generated resistance and ill will throughout his presidency. His nationalist leanings, which identified nature as a catalyst to reawaken the pioneer spirit—

demonstrated through his favorite pastime of hunting—made him appear to naturalists as bloodthirsty. At times he seemed to relish in the conflicts to preserve the environment, particularly when Congress believed he was usurping its power. When he signed the Antiquities Act into law in 1906, it gave him virtually unlimited power to establish any federal land as a national monument; his declaration of the Grand Canyon as such incensed mining industries and Congress, but pleased preservationists.[112] Even in the most innocuous of circumstances, such as the president's message of forest conservation to school children on Arbor Day in 1907, he seemed to go out of his way to denigrate those who disagreed with his position. Employing biblical allusion, he chastised "any nation which in its youth lives only for the day, reaps without sowing, and consumes without husbanding, must expect the penalty of the prodigal whose labor could with difficulty find him the bare means of life."[113]

Roosevelt's indictment of corporate interests that exploited the environment reached a fever pitch in 1908. In a special message to Congress in January of that year, Roosevelt railed against "the man who makes an enormous fortune by corrupting legislatures and municipalities and fleecing his stockholders and the public." He likened corporate owners to common criminals, as both "stand on the same evil eminence of infamy." He warned the "powerful financier, the powerful politician, [and] the rich land thief" that "no matter how high their station," the "Federal Government does scourge sin" and put evildoers behind bars.[114] Roosevelt-the-cowboy, forever interested in frontier justice, threatened dishonest forces and invoked his posse—the national government—as the means to see justice done. This naturally inflamed the targets of his posse.

For several years, Roosevelt had offered multiple rationales for safeguarding the environment. He confused allies with seemingly contradictory behavior—hunter versus lover of nature, and conservationist versus preservationist. He entertained the public with his frequent and harsh broadsides against corporate interests, but perhaps not informed it well enough about the integral nature of the environment in the country's future.[115] He needed to find a way to appease the varied interests involved, to ensure that the protection and use of natural resources remained foremost in the nation's mind, and to confirm that he and the federal government rightfully held the authority to manage the environment. To that end, he brought some unique ideas to the presidency as to how and when the chief executive could execute his institutional and rhetorical power.

Three

Roosevelt and the Modern Rhetorical Presidency

Senator Mark Hanna's indictment of Theodore Roosevelt as a "damned cowboy" revealed his concern about the potential for Roosevelt's recklessness as president. Part of Hanna's worry stemmed from the deep friendship that he had enjoyed with President McKinley, and the fear that Roosevelt would deviate substantially from his friend's policies.[1] According to Roosevelt himself, he decided to be quite conservative as a new chief executive, in that he would be beholden to the previous executive's wishes. He reflected on this in his autobiography published several years after he left office. He stated that he had planned to "continue unchanged McKinley's policies for the honor and prosperity of the country," and asked McKinley's cabinet members to stay on in his administration. But he also made clear that he was not interested in becoming a "pale copy" of his predecessor, as he needed the flexibility to adapt to "new problems that arose."[2]

Roosevelt used his autobiography as a means to recount his philosophy for the presidency, perhaps hoping to reshape the perception of his actions while he had resided in the White House. For him, the government needed to become more efficient in its duty to advance the national interest, and it fell to the president to oversee that directly. Thus, he outlined three guiding principles that he had followed, and that he believed subsequent presidents should also heed: active management in governing, moral arbitration of policies, and regular engagement with legislators and the public. Most important, these principles became part of the foundation for what would later be described as the rhetorical presidency.

TR AND HIS THREE PRINCIPLES OF LEADERSHIP

Roosevelt craved action and so his first principle of vigorous governmental management reflected that. He declared that the president needed to be a "steward of the people" who would "actively and affirmatively" do what he could to safeguard the national welfare. He dismissed the notion that the president's power was limited to what he had "specific authorization" to do. He believed that his duty demanded that he do "anything" to meet the nation's needs. "Under this interpretation," he mused in his autobiography, "I did and caused to be done many things not previously done by the President. . . . I acted for the public welfare. . . . I did not care a rap for the mere form and show of power; I cared immensely for the use that could be made of the substance." For that reason, he pulled land from the public domain to protect forests. He justified his actions by calling on beloved past presidents such as Abraham Lincoln and Andrew Jackson, who he claimed read the Constitution in the same way that he did—unless it "explicitly forbid" them, it charged chief executives to "render the service" necessary to serve the people. It was not, he warned, a "straitjacket cunningly fashioned to strangle growth" by limiting the active exercise of presidential power for the greater good. He chided those who read the Constitution in a narrow, old-fashioned way that placed the president as the "servant of Congress." He reminded his readers that his interpretation must have been valid since the Supreme Court had dismissed the many legal and congressional challenges to his environmental stewardship.[3]

Roosevelt's activism in service to the general welfare highlighted his second presidential principle—the need for upright character. Roosevelt preached routinely about morality as a foundation for political service and national life.[4] He called for "absolute fitness, including honesty," to be the bedrock of his presidency. His autobiography recounted how he filled positions in his administration. He took recommendations from congressmen and, if someone deceived him about the "given class of qualifications" of a nominee, he refused to take any more suggestions from that congressman. Roosevelt was rare in how far he would go to uphold what he considered a moral stance. For example, he abhorred wrongdoers of any skin color and sided with disenfranchised cultures he believed were being morally wronged. He recalled an incident while he was president involving "Indian land." White settlers and congressional lawmakers advanced a bill that would allow some Native American land to be sold at $1.50 an acre. Roosevelt refused to sign the legislation and demanded that it be amended to five dollars an acre. "We sold that land under sealed bids," he noted, "and realized for the Kiowa, Comanche, and Apache Indians more than four million dollars—three millions and a quarter more than they would have obtained if I had signed the bill in its original form." President Roosevelt intervened on Native Americans' behalf on several such occasions.[5] He held some of the same racist thoughts about them as other early twentieth-century people, but he also believed that if they were treated fairly (by his definition), they could make meaningful contributions to the nation's culture.[6]

Roosevelt's moral crusade readied the government to "enforce the laws in aggressive fashion" against unscrupulous foes who abused them. He noted with some pride that when he took office, "it was a common and bitter saying that a big man, a rich man, could not be put in jail. We put many big and rich men in jail."[7] In overseeing the public's welfare he realized his third presidential principle—directly engaging constituencies both inside and outside Congress.

Roosevelt observed the difficulties in advancing national concerns when political parties demonstrated a "State's rights fetish." When that occurred, they forgot that the "Nation is supreme over State, county, and town alike." He admitted that he tried to work with such congressmen, and, to some extent, they tried to work with him. But due to the increasing friction and subsequent delays in pushing forward his environmental agenda, he adopted a distinctive strategy. Roosevelt remembered that he was "forced to abandon the efforts to persuade [Congress] to come my way, and then I achieved results only by appealing over the heads of the Senate and House leaders." In fact, Roosevelt's penchant for going around Congress allowed him to assemble a large coterie of non-legislative supporters who helped him steward the nation. The blue-collar and professional advocates—from magazines, businesses, and farms—whom he reached out to supported his agenda and helped give him the power to get things done. He gave particular thanks to the "leading newspaper correspondents at Washington [who] were as a whole a singularly able, trustworthy, and public-spirited body of men, and the most useful of all agents in the fight for efficient and decent government." According to him, with newspapers carrying his messages, he demonstrated that he could "arouse public attention" and sometimes "force" his position to be accepted by Congress.[8]

Roosevelt's dynamic form of presidential leadership at the beginning of the modern era reverberated throughout the century and into the next with his successors. For some contemporary scholars, however, presidential activism to the extent Roosevelt engaged in proved disquieting, if not downright dangerous.

INTERPRETING RHETORICAL LEADERSHIP

In their pivotal essay published in 1981, James Ceaser, Glen Thurow, Jeffrey Tulis, and Joseph Bessette coined and discussed the term "rhetorical presidency." According to them, the evolution of the mass media at the turn of the twentieth century gave presidents the ability to reach wider audiences. In particular, it provided the presidencies of Theodore Roosevelt and Woodrow Wilson the ability to use "popular rhetoric" as a means of governing. "Popular leadership through rhetoric," they alleged, "was suspect" because early chief executives, such as George Washington, "seldom" spoke directly to the populace. Even when early presidents did speak directly to citizens, they noted, it strictly involved issues related to the Constitution, matters of war, and general patriotism—not matters of policy. The supposed reserved nature of Roosevelt's predecessors appeared consistent with the original intent of the Founding Fathers: those men "looked with great suspicion on popular rhetoric" with its tendency to devolve into demagoguery and pernicious likelihood to short-circuit the reasoning process. Ceaser et al. noted that the Constitution's framers understood that "popular rhetoric" could not be "entirely avoided," but that presidents needed to use it sparingly to minimize governance through the engagement of the public's "transient opinion" and fickle "mood." This team of political and government scholars concluded that the presidential rhetoric that "has a nice ring but a hollow sound," and the "oratory that swelled popular expectations . . . [beyond] what government could possibly achieve," proved a disservice to the nation. While they acknowledged that a president's uplifting rhetoric was needed occasionally, too much of it distorted the balance between the need for hope and the will for pragmatism.[9]

As mentioned in Chapter One, Tulis expanded the assessment of Roosevelt in his book, *The Rhetorical Presidency*. He reached several conclusions about the president's leadership. First, he labeled Roosevelt the "father of the rhetorical presidency." According to Tulis, Roosevelt initiated the practice of attempting to generate public support with his popular rhetoric, bypassing Congress in the process. Second, Roosevelt's popular rhetoric consisted solely of his speeches, such as his inaugural addresses, or those campaign-like speeches the president gave during his "swings around the circle"—multistop tours he took to make his case for some type of legislation prior to congressional deliberations. Third, Roosevelt embraced "demagoguery in its worst guises" as a way to stem the "blatant appeals to passion" that was rife from other political agents attacking his positions. Like his colleagues, Tulis admitted that the rhetorical presidency had its good points but, on balance, it proved "more deleterious than beneficial . . . because [it] is not just the use of popular leadership, but rather the routine appeal to public opinion." In other words, popular rhetoric became a "crisis tool" for presidents to frame situations, other than war or extreme economic depression, as an emergency to generate support; with repeated use, the public would be unable to "distinguish genuine from spurious crises."[10]

Ceaser, Tulis, and others have tended to cast popular leadership and the rhetorical presidency in largely narrow terms. As later scholars have demonstrated, presidents well before Roosevelt recognized the need to go public. Iconic chief executives such as George Washington and Thomas Jefferson, and less heralded presidents such as Franklin Pierce and Rutherford B. Hayes, engaged in direct relationships with their respective publics (albeit not in the same ways and frequency that Roosevelt could due to more advanced technologies available and changing cultural expectations).[11]

As Martin J. Medhurst noted particularly about Tulis's work, limiting the expression of a rhetorical presidency to "spoken discourse, directed to popular audiences, on matters of policy, for the purpose of forcing Congress to act without due deliberation," disguises the fact that rhetoric, and its performance, functions much more broadly. According to Medhurst, rhetoric manifests in any symbolic act, focusing on multiple types of constituencies, pertaining to a range of occasions, and achieving a multitude of goals.[12] Such a "rhetorical being," Medhurst alleged, approached communicative engagement in flexible and broad ways that belied any real or imagined dictates of office.[13]

This expansive understanding of a president as a "rhetorical being" provides a more illuminating explanation for many of Roosevelt's actions outside the traditionally conceived construct of a rhetorical president. For example, Roosevelt engaged in two non-speech events unrelated to the passage of specific environmental policy or the act of going over the head of Congress. These instances represented a unique rhetorical means to communicate ideas about his authority and the ecological issues facing the nation.

In the summer of 1902, thousands of United Mine Workers went on strike against an association of anthracite coal mine owners, representing what Roosevelt biographer Edmund Morris called the "greatest labor stoppage in history." Roosevelt initially decided that he could not intervene in a private dispute between workers and their employers. After several months of tempers flaring between the parties and increasing violence and bloodshed, and with winter approaching, he became the first president to invite labor leaders and mine owners to the White House so that he could mediate their stalled negotiations. Because of his intervention, the parties reached a settlement; but if they had been too stubborn, Roosevelt had already made constitutionally questionable plans to use the military to take ownership of the mines and force union members back to work as government employees.[14] Even without a direct speech to the public asking for its support, Roosevelt showed the power of the presidency regarding an environmental issue—media reporting of his private actions communicated the importance of presidential management of the coal industry and the importance of that resource for national wellbeing.

Roosevelt's other non-speech event related to the environment appeared both amusing and unsettling for the nation. Late in his second term, he engaged in a public battle with a private citizen, one William Long. According to Roosevelt biographer William Harbaugh, "All the president could gain was the satisfaction of speaking his mind, and he could gain that only by compromising the dignity of his office."[15] Roosevelt publicly objected to nature writers like Long, whom Roosevelt believed anthropomorphized nature and who treated their accounts as scientific fact. Furthermore, he disagreed vehemently with such writers who argued that nature provided an escape from everyday responsibilities: going back to nature, for the president, meant using the wilderness as a catalyst to reinvigorate the body and spirit and not turning your back on the opportunities in civilization.[16]

President Roosevelt attacked Long in an interview that appeared in the summer 1907 issue of *Everybody's Magazine*. The interview opened with the president's "outrage" at natural history "fables" being used in schools to teach scientific facts. He turned his ire specifically on Long, calling him the "worst of these nature-writing offenders" with his stories about wolves containing the "wildest improbabilities and a few mathematical impossibilities." According to Roosevelt, when Long asserted that a wolf kills a caribou by biting through its heart, the wolf had to have "either turned a somersault . . . or else got his head upside down under the fore legs of the fawn, a sufficiently difficult performance." Roosevelt feared the effect of such fantastically untrue stories on his environmental agenda:

> "The preservation of the useful and beautiful animal and bird life of the country depends largely upon creating in the young an interest in the life of the woods and fields. If the child mind is fed with stories that are false to

> nature, the children will go to the haunts of the animals only to meet with disappointment. The result will be disbelief, and the death of interest."[17]

Long fired back in *The New York Times* the day after Roosevelt's interview appeared. He called the attack by the president "venomous in spirit" and denigrated Roosevelt's intellectual ability as a naturalist.[18] A day later, Long released a private letter he had sent to the president that was again the focus in the news media. Long echoed the Founding Fathers concern about a president's need to be circumspect when engaging with the public: he wrote that Roosevelt had "used the advantage of [his] high position to injure him." The nature writer labeled the "foolish words" of the president in "bad taste" and notable for their "cowardice."[19] For weeks Long sent information to *The New York Times* and other newspaper outlets that attempted to substantiate his work, dismiss Roosevelt's natural history observations, and to denounce the president as a wanton killer of wildlife.[20]

Much to the delight of journalists, Roosevelt responded publicly. His article, "Nature-Fakers," appeared in *Everybody's Magazine* in September 1907. He stated his "contempt both for the men who invented preposterous fiction about wild animals, and for the credulous stay-at-home people who accepted such fiction as fact." But he levied a withering indictment against Long, calling him the "most reckless and least responsible" of the nature fakers whose information about animal behavior and intelligence were "comic absurdities." According to Roosevelt, Long and others engaged in not just literary license but "yellow journalism of the woods" that constituted "deliberate perversion of fact." He noted that the true study of nature reflected a preservationist mindset: it provided a "real knowledge and appreciation of wild things, of tree, flowers, birds, and . . . of the wilderness," which in turn gave "an added beauty and health to life."[21] *The New York Times* headline the day after the president's article, "ROOSEVELT WHACKS DR. LONG ONCE MORE," along with supportive editorials of the article, signaled the end of the nature faker controversy.[22]

However unorthodox it was to mediate between business owners and employees, and to begin a public name-calling spat with a private citizen, Roosevelt's execution of what he believed as his presidential duty represented a form of rhetorical leadership. Such leadership revolved around the classical notion of prudence, in that he needed to perform the "right balance between . . . virtues of thought and character."[23] Roosevelt demonstrated his "virtue of thought" by using experts like Gifford Pinchot to help him make policy, and calling repeatedly for scientific accuracy in natural history study. Along with his perceived cowboy-like persona that oversaw judicial indictments of various political evildoers, and his fervent belief in taking the moral high ground against pseudo-educators and their outright dissembling about nature, he clearly communicated his righteousness of character. Roosevelt acknowledged in his autobiography the need to be prudentially insightful—to be rhetorical—as he "was content to wait and see what method might be necessary in each given case as it arose" when prosecuting his presidential duties.[24]

Moreover, Roosevelt's public performance of possessing good sense and a good heart worked to crystallize the "presidency as the dominant interpretive force in American national politics." According to Mary Stuckey, Roosevelt's administration spearheaded the thrust toward an "institutionalized primacy" as the president unabashedly attempted to seize the argumentative high ground and call into question the congressional will to guide the nation.[25] The president's creative uses of rhetoric provided opportunities for his ascendant leadership as the chief interpreter of environmental matters beyond that occurring, or not, in the halls of Congress.

Of course, legislative leaders and many American citizens seemed to have had enough of Roosevelt's rhetorical antics by the end of his second term. His infamous maneuver to secure millions of acres of trees from use before signing legislation that would prevent him from doing just that incensed Congress. He reveled in Congress's reaction when recounting the event years later: "The opponents of the Forest Service turned handsprings in their wrath; and dire were their threats against the Executive."[26] Legislators uttered cries of "governmental landlordism" and "Executive Despotism" because of Roosevelt's action, while some political and business leaders in the West murmured "sentiments of secession." Because of the acrimonious relationship between the branches, Congress looked for any way it could to stymie the president. It found one when Roosevelt asked for funds to be allotted to the Inland Waterways Commission and to the National Country Life Commission. The former planned to survey the nation's rivers and develop a plan to improve them, and the latter intended to research farm production so that recommendations could be developed to improve production. Not only did Congress refuse to fund these organizations, even after they had submitted their reports, but it even refused the funds necessary to print the reports.[27]

Roosevelt acknowledged that Congress's intransigence was not the only problem. According to him, business people and the general public believed that the natural environment was a source of infinite resources and seemed unaware of the "relation of the conservation of natural resources to the problems of National welfare and National efficiency." He wrote in his autobiography:

> "[The] public resources were being handled and disposed of in accordance with the small considerations of petty legal formalities, instead of for the large purposes of constructive development. . . . The place of the farmer . . . was still regarded solely as that of a grower of food . . . while the human needs and interest of himself and his wife and children still remained wholly outside the recognition of the Government. . . . [The] need for forest protection in the East had not yet begun to enter the public mind."

As long as the nation remained misinformed, it would be lethargic in its support to manage the environment properly. Roosevelt chastised the public and the politicians for only seeming to engage in conservation initiatives in roundabout ways, in a "disconnected series of pork-barrel problems, whose only real interest was in their effect on the reelection or defeat of a Congressman here and there."[28] This toxic combination of public ignorance and private greed, along with congressional vindictiveness spurred on by Roosevelt's combativeness, seemed tailor-made for a new rhetorical strategy.

THE INSTITUTIONAL AND RHETORICAL FOUNDATIONS FOR THE GOVERNORS' CONFERENCE

Late in his presidency, Roosevelt looked for a way to address the issues of environmental regulation in a deliberately managed, authoritatively affirming, and a compellingly communicated fashion. He found it in the organization and production of the Governors' Conference. This gathering of the nation's leaders and thinkers in May 1908 provided him a forum to popularize the need for protection of natural resources in a way never before seen. In addition, it gave him the chance to rehabilitate his own controversial image as a usurper of legislative power (such as when his "midnight proclamations" stymied Congress's desire to rob him of his ability to preserve forest areas), and to soften his image as a bully (such as when he publicly browbeat naturalist and private citizen William Long).

Roosevelt's taking his case public in such a grand manner, at first glance, might resemble the traditional conception of the rhetorical presidency. As Ceaser et al. might argue, a president who resorted to "popular leadership" planned to use "emotional appeals to ignorant audiences" and to substitute "symbolic action" for actual political policy negotiations.[29] But the Governors'

Conference went far beyond such a misinformed understanding of the rhetorical presidency. The conference was not so much a direct appeal to the public but rather an opportunity to open a window on legislative discussions about the environment. The conference featured scores of some of the most learned and successful people in the nation discussing conservation and governmental control—a far cry from notions of "emotional appeals to ignorant audiences." Finally, given the conference's format providing opportunities for policy wrangling, the consequences from the event attained both symbolic levels and practical ends. In other words, Roosevelt planned not to upend the presidency, despite warnings of that institution's supposed turn to the rhetorical. Instead, he planned to reify its institutional authority while attempting to open a space for debate about conservation.

Roosevelt demonstrated the practical application of his principles of presidential leadership by employing three tools for the promotion and organization of the conference: the mass media; the trappings of a particular type of presidential speech; and a specific, mythic storyline that overturned his previous articulations of such stories.

First, Roosevelt capitalized on the mass media. As Ceaser et al. noted, the technology of the day allowed the president to reach far more people than previous chief executives could; journalists, though, acted as "filters in the communication process" and thereby shaped how the public interpreted messages.[30] Roosevelt, however, chose not to be a passive part of that process. He wanted to control what was printed. According to historian George Juergens, Roosevelt ingratiated himself in journalists' good wishes when he noticed a "cluster of sodden newsmen huddled" outside the White House in 1902 and invited them in, turning a small room near his study into an official press corps room. The president's largesse came with conditions. The publicity he wanted to generate for himself needed his approval before those journalists could write about it.[31]

For the most part, journalists kowtowed to Roosevelt's will. Some did so out of affection as they viewed the president as a learned "member of their tribe," a man who was a known bibliophile and accomplished author in his own right.[32] David Barry, a journalist during the early twentieth century and Roosevelt supporter, chronicled the interaction of the president with the mass media. Barry lauded him for knowing the "value and potent influence of a news paragraph written as he wanted it written." In fact, "Mr. Roosevelt did not hesitate . . . to suggest news articles and news paragraphs to the reporters, and even went so far on more than one occasion as to write out with his own hand what he wanted sent over the wire."[33] Certain news magazines, in competition to secure the most subscribers, loved it when the president wrote articles for them, and particularly enjoyed the fact that he made such colorful copy for their own stories.[34] Other journalists followed the president's lead since he was known to contact editors and demand that a journalist be fired for a breach of honor, real or imagined. He exploited a mass media still in its infancy, one unsure of how to negotiate the power imbalance between it and the president, in ways that his successors could not have dreamt doing.[35]

This proved critical regarding his plan to promote the significance of the Governors' Conference and to elevate his diminishing reputation as a responsible leader. He needed the journalists' goodwill, and their fear of him, so that they would allow him to shape the coverage of his event and position it as an affirmation of his presidential authority.

Second, with the multitude of forces arrayed against Roosevelt, and the charges that he exceeded presidential authority on many occasions, he ensured that the unprecedented Governors' Conference resembled another common presidential occasion—the State of the Union. That annual event privileged the president's role as a rhetorical leader. The Constitution directs the president to report regularly, in the form of an annual message, on the state of the nation and the policies needed to make it stronger. The annual message provided the chief executive an important advantage. As a distinctive genre, Karlyn Campbell and Kathleen Jamieson noted, it "helps to maintain the role of the executive," in that the president has sole responsibility to deliver the message to Congress. "By the sheer fact of its delivery," they wrote, "the address reminds the country that presidents have a unique role in our system of government," as they command a "national vantage point" in which to assess the problems facing the country and to direct attention toward the solutions. Although George Washington and John Adams delivered their messages orally, from Thomas Jefferson through Roosevelt, presidents wrote their messages. Woodrow Wilson reestablished the oral delivery of the president's annual messages in person. From Wilson on, members of Congress, the Supreme Court justices, and the public gathered in the president's presence to hear him and tacitly affirm the importance and legitimacy of his authority.[36]

During the first week of each December, Roosevelt sent a written message to the Senate and the House fulfilling his constitutional duty. His messages typically covered about three-dozen topics including, but not limited to, labor relations, foreign trade, military preparations, and immigration. The Governors' Conference borrowed the format of the State of the Union to give Roosevelt an advantage. Although the conference was in May, it called for the assemblage of Congress and other key audiences in the presence of the chief executive to hear him speak, essentially echoing a constitutionally mandated format that would become commonplace in later presidencies. In employing this format, with some modifications regarding the guest list, those in attendance implicitly sustained the right for Roosevelt to speak on a singular topic regarding the state of the nation's health, and to consider his remedies for it.

Third, as a genre, the State of the Union speech contains several interlocking and recurring themes. These include presidents constructing a collective national character with a public discussion of the values undergirding American identity; seeking to connect the past and the present to guide the audience to understand how it has arrived at its current predicament; and providing policy recommendations that emerge out of the previous themes. Campbell and Jamieson observed that the constitutional dictate for the delivery of the State of the Union address places the president in the "role of national historian," allowing him the opportunity to "involve Congress and the people in an affirmation that this is not only the way it was, but also the way it will be."[37] The State of the Union's focus on the past and the present privileged a form of communication that Roosevelt was fond of utilizing—mythic narrative.

Myths represented the final tool Roosevelt employed to demonstrate rhetorical leadership. He routinely used a particular one—the Frontier Myth—to advance his political agenda across topics ranging from race to women's equality, and military engagement.[38] The Frontier Myth represented an ideologically simple narrative cast with larger-than-life backwoods heroes engaged in fantastic adventures on an untamed North American continent. He had published a well-received, mythic history of cultural and environmental advancement in the 1890s. His multi-volume *The Winning of the West* reached back into America's past to find a pristine state of nature to cherish, to identify the men and women who conquered it as fulfillment of God's will, and to reveal the subsequent development of American culture.[39] His historical work popularized the wondrous nature of the frontier. This world-building story—offered in Frederick Jackson Turner's treatise but commercialized by mass media advocates such as Roosevelt—explained America's political, economic, and social progress, at the expense of Native Americans and nature, as simple cosmic destiny.

Roosevelt's novelized, mythic history, with his vivid descriptions of idealistic settings and stalwart characters, reflected his belief in the power of the environment to undergird the development of national character. He marveled at the boundless vistas eighteenth-century settlers of all types found upon setting foot in the new world. "Where the rivers ran, their alluvial bottoms were densely covered with trees . . . and were often overflowed in the spring freshets. Sometimes the prairies were long . . . [and] so broad as to be a day's journey across . . . the stretches of grass-land seemed limitless."[40] The trepidation that newcomers undoubtedly felt came through the pages of Roosevelt's history as he described the perpetual gloom provided by vast forests. "The sunlight could not penetrate the roofed archway of murmuring leaves," he wrote, "through the gray aisles of the forest men walked always in a kind of midday gloaming. . . . All the land was shrouded in one vast forest. It covered the mountains from crest to river-bed, filled the plains." Swarming with game such as the "shaggy-maned herds of unwieldy buffalo," "round-horned elk," and the "extraordinarily numerous" bears, wolves, and deer, Roosevelt described early American pioneers as subsistence hunters who had no choice but to kill animals for food and use trees to make crude housing.[41] His retelling of American history in *The Winning of the West* celebrated the magnificence of a largely untouched continent whose inhabitants used the environment in limited fashion.

Just as mythic narratives call for otherworldly foes to battle upright heroes, Roosevelt's retelling of America's origin featured Native Americans as antagonists. He focused on the need to remove them because he believed they were indifferent to utilizing environmental resources as a civilized nation would. They had to be conquered, he justified in *The Winning of the West*, because they had no real "governmental system" in which to negotiate for land. Otherwise, he mused, it would be a "warped, perverse, and silly morality which would forbid a course of conquest that has turned whole continents into the seats of mighty and flourishing civilized nations" to allow the unrealized use of the natural world for uncultured groups of tribes.[42] Despite his romanticized vision of a largely unspoiled frontier, and the life-and-death battles between mythic antagonists, the environment had to be used.

Roosevelt, like Turner, credited the struggles in the mythic environment for the birth of the American progenitor:

> "Settlers were men of sterling worth, fit to be the pioneer fathers of a mighty and beautiful State. They possessed the courage that enabled them to defy outside foes, together with the rough, practical common sense that allowed them to establish a simple but effective form of government. . . . The pioneers were hunters and husbandmen. Each, by the aid of the axe and brand, cleared his patch of corn land in the forest, close to some clear, swift-flowing stream, and by his skill with the rifle won . . . the game on which his family lived until the first crop was grown."[43]

Thanks to books such as *The Winning of the West* popularizing political and historical theory, the Frontier Myth had become a compelling, culturally embedded explanation for the nation's rise to prominence.[44]

Given how much Roosevelt had used this mythic narrative over much of his adult life to promote his political ideas, it comes as no surprise that he would consider turning to it again for the foundation of his speech at the Governors' Conference. And that was the problem he faced.

Roosevelt's frequent use of the Frontier Myth had painted him into a corner. His own articulation of that myth for decades focused on *using* the land—in limited ways for simple survival and in grandiose ways as examples of American power. Over time, the myth's divine articulation of rugged individuals conquering the environment to establish a nation had become linked in the social imagination with wholesale abuses perpetrated by individual land speculators, corrupt politicians, and cut-and-run loggers for the material ease of an apathetic populace. The Frontier Myth that Roosevelt frequently used now appeared inconsistent with his call for environmental protection. He needed to alter the myth in a way that would still allow him to use its explanatory and compelling narrative power.

Although myths may act to preserve a cultural system, they can be changed to usher in a new status quo. Advocates calling for a change in political realities can use one myth to contest another myth's legitimacy. According to Bruce Lincoln, a new myth challenges the "credibility of a given myth," reducing its historical stature and denying it the "capacity to continually reconstruct accustomed social forms." In the process, the new myth reinterprets the narrative details the culture had embraced in the old myth to establish new benchmarks for national progress. Any changes in a world-building mythic narrative, Richard Slotkin wrote, would need significant adjustments in the key elements of that myth—specifically the key elements of the major protagonists and the setting in which they existed—to effect enough change in the traditional narrative. This change reorients the audience's understanding and acceptance of its new identity in the significantly altered myth.[45]

In his Governors' Conference address, Roosevelt substantially modified the Frontier Myth. His new story now challenged the accepted truths about the American pioneer, the unlimited universe of resources, and the contradictory policies that had sprung up to manage the environment. Along with his near takeover of mass media to trumpet the conference as a unique and important example of presidential leadership before, during, and after the event, he succeeded in embedding the idea of conservation in the national consciousness.

Four

The Governors' Conference

Throughout his career, Roosevelt tried to educate lawmakers and the public about the need to protect the environment. Despite his presidential initiatives involving "midnight proclamations" and public scourging of "nature fakers," he recognized that his ideas had not always received sustained, coherent, and celebratory attention by the media.

Years before the Governors' Conference, President Roosevelt called for scientific management and comprehensive policymaking to guide the wise use of the environment. One notable occasion for this call occurred at a meeting of the Society of American Foresters. This organization had been created in 1901 by Gifford Pinchot to assist the members of his new Bureau of Forestry (which had begun as the somewhat smaller Forestry Division in the Department of Agriculture). The mission of the society involved furthering the "cause of Forestry in America by fostering a spirit of comradeship among foresters," and providing forums for the exchange of ideas related to forestry. Pinchot held weekly meetings at his home and invited Roosevelt to speak. The president accepted and attended a meeting in March 1903. According to Pinchot, Roosevelt's speech "did very much to stimulate the spirit of devotion to their work among the men who heard him."[1]

At that meeting, Roosevelt gratefully acknowledged the service to the country that those foresters were performing with their "scientific study and practical application . . . of improved methods" to preserve wooded areas. He also acknowledged that protecting the forests did not mean they were off-limits—"wise use" allowed forests to be used by the "settler, the rancher, the miner, the man who lives in the neighborhood, and indirectly the man who may live hundreds of miles off." Forests appeared pivotal as he declared, "Forest protection alone can maintain the streamflow necessary for irrigation in the West. . . . The relation between forests and the whole mineral industry is an extremely intimate one, for mines cannot be developed without timber."[2] By connecting these separate environmental issues together, he not only elevated the importance of the Forestry Bureau's efforts, but he also attempted to generate backing for their efforts across a spectrum of seemingly disparate interests.

Beyond the scientific practicality of the Society of American Foresters' work, Roosevelt charged them with another duty. He told them that their "usefulness to the body politic" came when they were able to "instil [sic] your own ideals into the mass of your fellowmen." In other words, he needed them to get the media to promote their work. Ironically, Roosevelt himself failed to get much media coverage. Despite the rarity of a sitting president delivering a speech at a private home (an example of both his active management style and regular engagement with the public), and attendance by a "distinguished company of scientists" as reported by one newspaper, few media outlets covered Roosevelt's appearance and those that did tended not to feature it on their front pages.[3]

The president attempted to generate media attention with other events. Just two months before his 1905 inauguration (after his landslide election in November 1904), he worked with Pinchot to transfer forest reserve management from the General Land Office to the Pinchot-controlled Bureau of Forestry. To help push congressional legislators to approve the transfer, Pinchot invited Roosevelt to speak at another event. This time Roosevelt was named as the Honorary President of the American Forest Congress (AFC). Members of the AFC—which included industry leaders from mining, timber, livestock, and railroads, as well as several legislators and spokesmen from governmental units responsible for reclamation and geology—met in Washington for a multi-day meeting in January 1905.[4]

During the president's speech to the AFC, he again focused on the interrelation of constituencies needed to bring about conservation. "For the first time the great business and the forest interests of the nation have joined together," he stated early in the speech, "to consider their individual and their common interests in the forest." That "common interest" rested on the notion of use; these people had come together to "consider how best to combine use with preservation," preservation that he strictly defined as the "promise for the forests of the future." Although he threatened any industry that destroyed resources unnecessarily, affirming that he was "against the land-skinner every time" as that person was a "curse . . . to the country," he also assured the gathered industries that he wanted "every portion of the public domain" given the "highest possible amount of use." This time Roosevelt highlighted a new idea he considered important. Near the end of his speech, he mentioned the need for business to cooperate with the government so that business could "do infinitely more for themselves than it would be possible for any government under the sun to do for them." Initially, it seemed as if business held the power in its relationship with government as Roosevelt appeared to render his organization powerless without industry cooperation. But he returned to this idea repeatedly, and each time it became clearer that federal government involvement would mean strict control and oversight of industry behavior.[5]

The AFC event generated more media attention than Roosevelt's visit to Pinchot's house, but most newspapers still positioned the story on its inner pages. Even the president's attack against the cursed "land-skinners" failed to bring much coverage. If the event did make the front page, such as in *The Norfolk Weekly News Journal*, it received only passing mention.[6] Perhaps frustrated with the paucity of journalistic interest, Roosevelt went directly to the media to trumpet his ideas about natural resource use, cooperation, and supervision.

In June 1907, Roosevelt visited Jamestown, Virginia, and spoke before the National Editorial Association. The crowd obviously gave him direct access to scores of journalists simultaneously, but the location also communicated a sense of myth. Jamestown represented the historic meeting place of Pocahontas and John Smith. That association between disparate legends provided a frontier truth: cooperation proved vital to survival and advancement.

Now Roosevelt asked for that collaboration between himself and the media. He lamented the fact that certain portions of Jamestown suffered from erosion by the James River.[7] The erosion had been the result of a public that "tended to live with an eye single to the present," and "permitted the reckless waste and destruction of much of our natural wealth." Stated another way, public indifference and industry leaders' practices had caused the erosion, and neither had the "foresight" to recognize the consequences of their actions; Roosevelt wanted the newspapers to highlight that. He called on members of the "public press . . . if they are really good servants of the people . . . to assail wrong-doing and wickedness." He wanted their cooperation with his crusade and for them to fulfill their duty to serve the public: they needed to keep the public informed about the unscrupulous forces that preferred "haphazard striving for immediate profit" and that disregarded the "foresight" of the government to develop the nation's resources.[8]

Strategically, Roosevelt used the mythic backdrop of Jamestown to foster a partnership with the media. He framed himself and the journalists in attendance as mythic heroes who had the responsibility to battle evildoers whose greed threatened the welfare of the nation. Perhaps to be expected, coverage of

Roosevelt's speech at the National Editorial Association event appeared as several lengthy, front-page stories.[9] Even without the mythic affiliation, though, reporters welcomed the opportunity to report on the president's words since he had acknowledged their power as "molders and guides of public thought."[10]

However, Roosevelt's public appearances as elements of his broadly conceived rhetorical presidency, and the mass media attention he received, may not have served the administration as well as he hoped. Environmental historian Samuel Hays noted that events like the American Forest Congress "did not create a sustained popular support which could help administration leaders persuade Congress to pass other measures."[11] Furthermore, Roosevelt's public engagements and blistering attacks played into what Tulis described as the "deleterious" effect of a rhetorical president.[12] For Tulis, such chief executives threatened to unbalance the constitutional power between the branches. Roosevelt's opponents may have seen his active engagement as an attempt to gain public authorization for his unilateral executive actions regarding the environment. His open revelry of his unfettered will, along with the power of his office, made it appear that he was all too ready to disregard institutional traditions and continue to move without Congress.

The questionable constitutionality of what he was ultimately planning aside, Roosevelt's unceasing goal involved educating people about the environment. The more coverage and concern he brought to the country's natural resources, the more leverage he could generate to parry congressional and business opposition—opposition that had been steadily growing in his second term. Thus, he needed a unique event that could capture the public's attention, allow him to push his agenda aggressively, and that still resembled a traditionally appropriate format for the deployment of presidential leadership. The organization and production of the Governors' Conference fit the bill.

CONSTRUCTING THE CONFERENCE IN THE NEWS

The Roosevelt administration's engagement of the mass media to promote the Governors' Conference began well before May 1908. In fact, Roosevelt decided to announce the conference during another much-heralded media event. The Inland Waterways Commission (IWC), attempting to publicize its own work in finding efficient ways to transport goods, embarked on a series of inspection tours of the country's lakes and rivers. "Roosevelt delightedly accepted an invitation," one biographer wrote, "to cruise down the Mississippi on a paddle steamer" with the IWC. The president recognized the importance of his involvement as he considered that particular river the "spiritual heart and the economic backbone" of the nation. By the time he boarded the USS *Mississippi* for his four-day trip in October 1907, several journalists accompanied him.[13] They, along with their shoreside colleagues, reported daily about the hordes of people who turned out to give their well-wishes to the president. Despite a downpour, *The Washington Herald* announced, "Thousands braved the elements along the line of the Presidential procession and gave the Executive a rousing cheer." *The Omaha Daily Bee* described the carnivalesque atmosphere at one stop in St. Louis, noting that "thousands of human throats" screaming for the president rivaled the "clanging bells" and the "thundering intonations of bursting bombs."[14] The multi-day coverage offered the public's affirmation of the president's trip—America's waterways needed attention.

At various stops along his river trip, Roosevelt chastised those who had neglected the "water highways," such as the railroad companies. As they prospered, people dependent on the river suffered. He declared in St. Louis that the entire country shared an "unhealthy" bent "toward the practically complete abandonment of the system of water transportation." Given the extent of the business lethargy that Roosevelt identified, it seemed natural that the federal government needed to oversee rehabilitation of processes related to the environment and the country's welfare. In Cairo, Illinois, he repeated the progressive call for national oversight where the "rights of the wage-worker" needed protection from those unscrupulous individuals who "amass great fortunes by speculating in and manipulating securities which are issued without any kind of control or supervision." Roosevelt put it simply: The future was at stake and only one institution had the power to bring it into existence and maintain the benefits for businesses, politicians, and "innocent people." The president seemed almost unable to resist jabbing at those who he believed stood against him, this time casting corporate and political leaders as representatives of an "evil eminence of infamy" in contrast to the hardworking laborer.[15]

Roosevelt's next stop, though, proved pivotal. Pinchot noticed that several state governors had joined the river trek. It prompted him to communicate an idea he had to the president. In order to bring the most attention to the country's natural resources, Pinchot argued that Roosevelt should invite every state governor to the White House and convene a conference about the environment.[16] Roosevelt embraced the idea. At the Memphis stop of the river trip, he offered criminal indifference as the reason for the conference. He again derided corporate interests for the crimes they committed by taking "public lands" for "private owners" who subordinated "home-making . . . to the desire for profit." Congress too found itself chastised for its "irregular and uncertain" deployment of resources to address environmental issues, which in turn discouraged the implementation of "far-reaching plans." By improving the country's waterways, other natural resources could be likewise improved. The extent of the issue led Roosevelt to declare that the "fundamental problem" facing America called for a solution that only the "whole Nation" could undertake. To that end, he announced that the Inland Waterways Commission had tasked him to "call a conference on the conservation of nature resources." He presaged that this event would "be among the most important gatherings in our history."[17]

Roosevelt achieved two ends with the announcement. Rather than antagonize critics with what could be considered as more "executive despotism" by his command for such a conference, the president shunted the responsibility for the conference to the Inland Waterways Commission. According to Douglas Brinkley, since everyone believed that "water was king," even the president's detractors had largely agreed with the creation and purpose of the IWC and would go along with its suggested gathering.[18] The president also set the stage for mandatory attendance at the conference since he had invited the "whole Nation" to participate in the "vital question to consider" for the country's "welfare;" failure to participate would mean failing to uphold national duty.

Roosevelt's announcement of the Governors' Conference was short; given that the idea was still in its embryonic stages, he did not go into great detail about it. While some media did mention the pronouncement, other Roosevelt-related news overshadowed it. Both the *Albuquerque Citizen* and *The Evening Star* pulled attention from the conference announcement by running front page cartoons of how bears reacted upon learning that the president was going to use his river trip to go hunting in the Louisiana canebrake. The *Albuquerque Citizen* cartoon showed a family of bears clearly upset, with one cub crying, "Run for your lives! Teddy is coming!" *The Evening Star's* contribution featured a bear dressed as Roosevelt scouting for his pack and warning them to stay quiet.[19] The other news that lessened the impact of the announcement involved stock market volatility and panic.[20] This time, *The Evening Star's* front-page cartoon showed Roosevelt aboard a paddle steamer trying to navigate around tree branches labeled "railroad trusts," "beef trusts," and "Standard Oil." The day after the president's Memphis speech, *The Washington Times* focused attention on Roosevelt's plan to "FIGHT BIG CORPORATIONS" that victimized innocent investors. Likewise, the *Bismarck Daily Tribune* reminded readers about Roosevelt's tendency to antagonize big business when its front-page headline blared, "ROOSEVELT MAKES BIG SPEECH AT DEEP WATER WAYS CONVENTION—IS SARCASTIC AT WALL STREET."[21]

Competing stories at the time of the announcement minimized the prominence of the governors' gathering. But Pinchot planned to get the news out about the conference. Appointed by Roosevelt to arrange the White House gathering, Pinchot employed a tactic that had already served him well. According to Stephen Ponder, "No aspect of publicity was more important to Pinchot than the creation of news for commercial newspapers and magazines." Pinchot knew that this "free publicity" had the potential to reach far larger audiences than government publications. His common practice involved peppering news organizations with "press bulletins"—stories that he and his staff wrote that summarized their research and conclusions formatted in news article style.[22] Like Roosevelt, who routinely wrote news stories himself, Pinchot's staff provided the mass media ready-made news about the Governors' Conference.

In mid-November 1907, newspapers carried a copy of the invitation Roosevelt sent to the governors. His letter began by claiming that America's current prosperity and population growth could be traced directly to nature's riches. As such, he appealed with "special force" to the "Governors . . . because of their close relations to the people and the responsibility for the welfare of their communities." The president publicly set the agenda for those governors who had previously railed against him—they needed to be concerned with the growing exhaustion of the very resources that he had claimed were the country's foundation for material success. Roosevelt's invitation to the governors also set the benchmark for the type of remarks to be made at the conference: "I shall invite a few recognized authorities to present brief descriptions of actual facts and conditions, without argument." Of course, the facts had already spoken, as the president noted that they had forced him "to believe that the conservation of our national resources is the most weighty question now before the people of the United States," and the "proposed conference, which is the first of its kind, will be among the most important gatherings in our history." Reflecting the seriousness of the conference, *The San Francisco Call* reported that the event would be no "mass convention;" instead, it would be a "quiet conference" between the president and his guests.[23] In other words, the conference would not be a public airing of blistering attacks from the president nor calls for his impeachment from governors, but a stately meeting between concerned leaders out to solve a national crisis together.

As news coverage of the Mississippi River trip demonstrated, the mass media's tendency to focus on Roosevelt as a sportsman and as a fire-and-brimstone preacher castigating industrial immorality made for colorful copy. Such copy tended to distract from the primary intent of the message.

With conference planning underway, Pinchot-provided news placed Roosevelt center stage—neither as a showman nor a demagogue—but as a chief executive whose performance would resemble and affirm his constitutional right to lead. The idea to invite the nation's governors (and up to three of their advisers) to Washington may have made the environment resemble a states' rights issue; different states had argued for different remedies for years. But the guest list ranged far beyond them. Similar to State of the Union addresses that would become common with later administrations, Roosevelt invited the members of Congress and the Supreme Court justices, thereby having all branches of government represented. Not only would the traditional setting indicate the need for dialogue between the executive and legislative branches, but the modern addition of the judicial branch would implicitly affirm the legality of policy arising from that dialogue.[24]

Given the outright warfare between himself and Congress this late in his presidency, Roosevelt needed symbols of collaboration to further his agenda. Invitations went out to a multitude of others, including: the president's cabinet; the Inland Waterways Commission membership; dozens of news reporters and magazine writers; representatives from professional associations involved with economics, manufacturing, health, agriculture, science, railroads, livestock, mining, farming, lumbering, engineering, medicine, and labor unions; and about fifty "general guests" from the Carnegie Foundation, the Smithsonian Institution, government bureaus, and universities. In his autobiography, Pinchot noted several "outstanding citizens" were "chosen to represent the people of the United States," including Democratic leader William Jennings Bryan, steel baron Andrew Carnegie, and railroad tycoon James Hill.[25] This congregation demonstrated that the environment was not simply a state's issue or a business concern. Gathering this many people from such varied walks of life signaled a cooperative assembly that had placed natural resources as a national subject.

Pinchot maneuvered the mass media to trumpet the news about the upcoming Governors' Conference. He shared a plethora of details about it that media diligently reported in the month before the event. The assemblage of leaders garnered the most press. Despite the guest list including foes of the president, *The Omaha Daily Bee* announced the conference to be a "love feast" between "men of the greatest divergence of views on politics and other questions" who will "join in a mighty chorus" expressing their support for Roosevelt's initiatives. The "Big Men" of the nation, *The Evening Star* stated, would join the president in the East Room of the White house for the "first time in the history of the country."[26] Several newspapers referred to the conference as "historic," "momentous," and the "most unique gathering that ever assembled in Washington." That language echoed the statements Roosevelt had made during his announcement of the conference months earlier, pointing to Pinchot's hand at supplying information to the press. The *New-York Tribune* provided a full, front-page pictorial of the participants attending the "remarkable conference"—Roosevelt surrounded by several notable foes, including governors from states that he had been battling, with all of them surrounded by pictures of workers harvesting natural resources.[27] The visual representation connected all the principal government agents and business leaders together, highlighting a cooperative relationship between them.

The media's constant claim about the unprecedented nature of the meeting led it to report on and to predict public opinion about the event. For example, the *Albuquerque Citizen* concluded that favorable public opinion was identified by the "great mass of correspondence which is pouring into the White House on this subject. Organizations of all sorts express realization of the greatness of the enterprise. . . . These letters are becoming of such volume that the stenographers at the White House are working overtime. . . . Information is constantly received [from] tourists from all parts of the country" planning to attend. With such interest, it proved no surprise that the "people of the country expect definite results of a far-reaching character" from the "great deliberative body" being convened.[28] The daily news coverage describing the nationwide interest in the event—citizens as sightseers or participants—again confirmed the Rooseveltian position that safeguarding natural resources was of interest and concern for the country.

Even the format and tools to be used at the conference became news. Journalists reported that Roosevelt would open the event and preside over it but that he would turn the hosting duties over to a different governor each day.[29] Governors, their advisers, and select individuals would present brief speeches during the three-day conference. As Pinchot recalled, speeches would not run too long as a bell ringer would communicate how much time remained for each speaker.[30] *The Washington Times* provided the minutiae related to the maps to be used: A platform "fifty two feet in length and nineteen feet high" was to be placed along one wall to allow for "two giant maps of the United States . . . the largest ever made by mechanical process," measuring "twelve by fifteen feet and . . . colored graphically, to show the various resources of the country."[31] Between the maps a device of "colored glass" hung that would depict various illustrations from the speeches to be given, including one that was a "glaring reproduction of a forest fire."[32] One newspaper predicted that the "labor and skill involved" to make these "hand-colored transparencies" visible for the participants meant that this method of presentation would be infrequently used in the future.[33] An "eagle of huge dimensions" stood near the maps with the US "coat of arms" visible as well.[34] Attendees would sit in "gilded chairs" in a room decorated with "green velvet, trimmed with gold rope."[35] No detail seemed too small to describe, particularly as the details pushed off the front-page reports about the antagonistic atmosphere that Roosevelt and many of the attendees had been fomenting for years.

Conspicuous with their absence from the extensive media coverage were the preservationist-minded advocates. According to the conference proceedings, out of the scores of public and private organizations invited, only two represented preservationist interests—the American Civic Association, and the American Scenic and Historic Preservation Society (ASHPS). The ASHPS representative spoke on the conference's last day, at the end of the day.[36]

Tellingly, not even Roosevelt's friend John Muir received an invitation due to the bitterness between Muir and Pinchot over the Hetch Hetchy controversy.[37] Muir sent a message to the president and the governors two weeks before the conference began. Speaking for the Sierra Club, Muir wanted the attendees to consider the "paramount value of scenic beauty among our natural resources," as the national body was not "dependent alone upon bread and water." According to Muir, the aesthetic proved more important than materiality, calling preservation the "greatest service that one generation can render to another." Rather than rely solely on a transcendentalist appeal, he even quantified what scenic beauty could mean to the nation: He noted that in Europe, tourists spent up to $550 million a year for nature's beauty and, if America left its natural resources untouched, it could make such profits too.[38]

However, the White House message appeared clear. Roosevelt's earlier, limited embrace of preservationists' rationales found no place at the conference. He failed to give any mention in his speech to protecting the environment for its beauty alone, nor for its tourist and sporting potential. And with the placement of the ASHPS representative's remarks at the very end of the program, preservationists appeared to have lost the president's support for their initiatives.

FRAMING ROOSEVELT'S ADDRESS

The event began like a royal coronation. "With a flourish of trumpets," *The Salt Lake Tribune* reported, the president entered the East Room of the White House at 11:00 a.m. on May 13. Complete with a "Marine band," the attendees jumped to their feet, clapped and shouted to the point that the recognition of Roosevelt became "tumultuous."[39] The proceedings began with a benediction by the Senate chaplain, part of which is included here:

> "The Lord thy God bringeth thee into a good land, a land of brooks of water, of fountains and springs, flowing forth in valley and hills, a land of wheat and barley and vines and fig trees. . . . Thou shalt not lack anything in it—a land where stones are iron and out of whose hills thou mayest dig copper. Beware lest when thou hast eaten and art full, thou forget the Lord thy God. . . . Yea, thy children shall possess the nations and make the desolate spots to be inhabited . . . . Thou hast made for us the Paradise through which these rivers flow. Now give us the strength of Thy Holy Spirit that we may go into this garden of Thine and bring forth fruit in Thy service."[40]

The Chaplain's blessing echoed several common themes, and particular ideas Roosevelt had already broached, regarding the environment. It affirmed the early pioneers' belief in the God-given bounty as represented by natural resources, and that such abundance appeared infinite since citizens would "not lack anything." It also dissuaded the preservationist thinking that the beauty of "Paradise" should be left untouched. This consecration called for Americans to cooperate together to use nature to "bring forth fruit." The benediction prepared the audience for Roosevelt's speech as he too would argue the necessity of resource use, but would disavow the notion of an infinite paradise. Use of the environment, though, needed guidance by some entity to ensure that use for generations yet unborn; the chaplain offered that advice with his warning of overeating (i.e., overuse of the natural resources).

While many considered Roosevelt a sort of preacher, he refrained from using the prayer as a bridge into arguing for the righteousness of a moral crusade for conservation. He instead grounded his address in the practicalities of the moment.

After the benediction, Roosevelt announced, "You have come hither at my request, so that we may join together to consider the question of the conservation and use of the great fundamental sources of wealth of this Nation."[41] He gave the attendees their agency by noting that he had simply made a "request" for participation; thus, they seemed concerned in their own right to work cooperatively with the administration. However, Roosevelt established his authority, and by virtue the federal government's, in a nuanced way. The media saturation of the conference's importance and the public's interest in it had left invitees little choice but to attend, and implicitly to side with the president by the act of their attendance. Newspaper and magazine readers had already been primed for the president and his administration to guide a national response to environmental abuse.

Further, if preservationist-minded attendees held out any hope that they still had presidential support, Roosevelt quickly disabused them of the notion that he stood vigorously with them. He embraced the business leaders' position that environmental resources were best considered as commercial prizes, as "fundamental sources of wealth," not as untouchable, picturesque gateways into spiritual communion with God.

By the sheer act of mounting the platform before his select audience, Roosevelt engaged his principles of leadership. His presence at the conference indicated his belief in the president's active role in governing and regular engagement with his constituencies. As he noted in his autobiography, he wanted to do things his predecessors had not, such as this unprecedented event, so that he could better serve the public will. In that sense Roosevelt used what he considered the public's desire for stewardship to justify his unorthodox but legally permissible action to consult with Congress about how the nation should be governed.[42] The policies that Roosevelt planned to discuss reflected his belief in fairness to the business and legislative interests involved, including outreach to the public who had likewise been invited to Washington.

The Governors' Conference worked to assuage tempers related to Roosevelt's perceived dismissal of Congressional authority. The event itself had been created in a constitutionally-recognized format—with modifications that would become commonplace with successive presidents—of a State of the Union speech with Congress, state legislators, and the public gathering to receive his report on the nation's health. Thus, Roosevelt legitimately acted as the nation's historian, just as presidents strive to do during a State of the Union event, and planned to recast the nation's mythic values in a way that could push his environmental agenda.

Thanks to Frederick Jackson Turner's essay and Roosevelt's own narrative histories, the North American frontier had become a place where the mythic origin of the country had been born. They both painted a portrait of early American heroes—people possessed of incredible strength who demonstrated resolute character and inventive thinking—who seemed destined to fulfill an otherworldly mandate to conquer an unlimited wilderness and become a nation unmatched by any other country. The Frontier Myth that Roosevelt spun years earlier had credited the challenges of the environment as the catalyst for America's forefathers to develop a democratic system of government. The values promoted in that myth favored those settlers whose body and mind allowed them to master their universe. Embedded myths like that one, though, can be transformed with other myths. Rhetors can offer amendments, what Slotkin referred to as "radical alterations," in the fundamental components of a myth—the protagonists, the scene, and the moral of the story. In doing so, the president planned to reconfigure the Frontier Myth and reorient his audience's understanding about what it meant for conservation.[43]

Roosevelt embedded the tripartite components of Slotkin's "radical alterations" into the typical State of the Union address, an address that fostered values, assessed information, and made recommendations to ensure the development of the nation.[44] Accordingly, the myth's protagonists embodied those values that reflected the nation's identity; the president's discussion of how the story's characters behaved represented a judgment about their values. The troubling scene of environment abuse in which the protagonists existed also called for assessment of it, with the president extending the survey of that scene from the ancient past to the near-term future. Finally, the new narrative that Roosevelt's speech offered contained the reconfigured agents and their universe. In other words, it provided a new account that contained the moral of the story—policy recommendations that could ensure the soundness of the state of the union.

REMAKING MYTH: THE PROTAGONISTS

Early in the speech, Roosevelt identified two new protagonists in his storyline. According to him, "for the first time in our history," the public witnessed a gathering of the states' governors to address the "vital" question of conservation. Those "chief executive officers" resembled the heroes of the Frontier Myth who had constituted a singular group of people acting in an unprecedented fashion to shape a continent. But even they were surpassed by another group. Roosevelt acknowledged that the representatives from scientific disciplines related to forestry, geology, and the like possessed a valuable trait—knowledge. They constituted the "experts" who were dedicated to the "development and use" of natural resources

The president subtly subordinated the governors and other legislators to his will as they seemed almost figureheads in his description, beholden to those people with access to facts about the environment. With the various commissions Roosevelt created, and Pinchot's attempt to professionalize the positions in those organizations, the federal government became merged with the scientific experts—*the* organization of learned thinkers and *the* repository for information—and could likely be seen as the most important factor in managing natural resources. The governors and congressmen's attendance made the conference a "meeting of the representatives of all the people of the United States," but only the "experts" could rightfully fix the "weightiest problem now before the Nation."

Introducing the conference attendees as new protagonists into an established narrative of American progress necessitated an adjustment of the old protagonists' status. The president disconnected the old heroes from their pedestal in the frontier story. Stated another way, he shifted the values attributed to early settlers' accomplishments to something less laudatory.

Rather than herald frontier pioneers as heroes, Roosevelt labeled them as "average." They were not "savages," nor were they fully civilized, he declared, but they constituted "very primitive peoples" interested "only with superficial natural resources"—those resources available only above ground. According to him, this marked them as regular people, not storybook legends. "Neither the primitive man nor the pioneer was aware of any duty to posterity in dealing with renewable resources." In retelling a portion of the frontier mythos, he relegated the once-lauded actions of those heroes to a display of their routine lack of knowledge: "When the American settler . . . exhausted the soil of his farm, he felt that his son could go West and take up another. The Kentuckian or the Ohioan felled the forest and expected his son to move west and fell other forests. . . . When the soil-wash from the farmer's field choked the neighboring river, the only thought was to use the railway rather than boats." The "average man," then, demanded "steadily increasing natural resources" to reach a higher level of civilization, a civilization he described as largely predicated on ignorance. This portrait depicted a substantially lesser notion of the frontier's rough-and-tumble masters. They may have possessed the great strength and fortitude that Roosevelt believed important to tame the frontier, but they also seemed to lack a basic understanding of their surroundings, a major counterpoint to their usual lionized depiction.

Not only did the fabled pioneers in the wilderness seem less in command of their surroundings than traditionally depicted in myth, Roosevelt further diminished their authority. He contrasted their importance with the political founders of the nation. The founders appeared to be cognizant of the need for judicious use of natural resources, so much so that they established a system of government around that concept.

The status of the Founding Fathers as the originators of America's government took on even greater meaning in Roosevelt's revised mythic history. He praised the founding fathers since they had possessed a trait the "average" pioneers lacked. He thought it remarkable that the founders who knew "so little" about the extent of the natural resources available still "exercised a wise forethought" about them. Roosevelt singled out George Washington for particular notice: "Washington clearly saw that the perpetuity of the States could only be secured by union, and that the only feasible basis of union was an economic one; in other words, that it must be based on the development and use of their natural resources. Accordingly, he helped to outline a scheme of commercial development, and by his influence an interstate waterways commission was appointed by Virginia and Maryland." Roosevelt argued that the existence of the United States stemmed not from the mythic notion of Puritans escaping to find religious freedom, but because one man—President Washington—had the farsightedness to embrace the importance of conservation.

Furthermore, the president connected himself and everyone in the East Room to that new history of America's progenitors and their goals. According to him, "It was in Philadelphia that the representatives of all the States met for what was in its original conception merely a waterways conference; but when they had closed their deliberations the outcome was the Constitution which made the States into a nation. The Constitution . . . grew in large part out of the necessity for united action in the wise use of one of our natural resources. The wise use of all of our natural resources . . . is the great material question of today." Just as Washington had created a commission to study waterways, so too had Roosevelt—the Governors' Conference itself had sprung from his Inland Waterways Commission. He made it clear that the country's founding was based on "commercial development" and not some aesthetic sense of godly beauty; the United States existed because it materially used the environment. He elevated the values of sagacity and commercialism above the subsistence-level ignorance exhibited by the "average" frontiersmen.

Mythically speaking, Roosevelt invoked what Mircea Eliade might call "Sacred Time"—the belief that certain pivotal and primordial points in history are cyclical and can reoccur in the present.[45] The conference participants, particularly Roosevelt, now stood equivalent to the nation's founders since each group had come together within their own eras—and each group had now come together even though separated by the centuries-long gulf of time—for "common effort" and "common action" to address the question of "wise use."

The president made other associations across time involving other well-known, sacred icons. While the Frontier Myth placed the significance of the nation's origin with the arrival of European settlers in the seventeenth century, Roosevelt connected the implication of that arrival to a time centuries before that. "When our forefathers met in Independence Hall," he stated, "Mining was carried on fundamentally as it had been carried on by the Pharaohs in the countries adjacent to the Red Sea." Roosevelt may have displaced the Puritans from America's mythic origin, offering instead President Washington's waterways commission as the catalyst for nation-building, but he still advanced a sacred understanding of the nation's history. He echoed the Puritans' belief in North America as a New Israel with his references to Pharaohs and the Red Sea (and implicitly Moses leading his people to a promised land), which created an earlier starting point in the nation's timeline. The biblical references gave him the means to maintain the allusion of America's sacred destiny without the direct presence of the "average" Puritan settlers.

Roosevelt invoked another set of hallowed pasts. "The wares of the merchants of Boston" in 1776, the president observed, "like the wares of the merchants in Nineveh and Sidon," were carried at sea in ships roughly similar between the two eras. For people familiar with these parts of the Bible, those two cities possessed special meaning. After his awakening in the great fish, Jonah visited the city of Nineveh to convince the people to renounce their ungodly materialistic desires; Sidon was a port city made wealthy by trading that Jesus visited, warning its citizens of their avariciousness.[46] Even with the Puritans "gone," America's origin encompassed ancient religious sources to confirm its supposed God-given destiny and communicate the dangers of materialism regarding uncontrolled use of natural resources.

By disconnecting the Puritan myth from the nation's founding, Roosevelt made a considerable alteration to the story. He instead offered conservation as the reason for the Constitution. Yet, he resisted destroying the religious framing for America's origin—that may have been too jarring a change. Instead, he simply shifted their ancestral protagonists starting point backwards. Roosevelt's stretching of the Frontier Myth's timeline gave him the means to alter substantially the importance of traditional frontier heroes. He spoke in measured terms about them, neither glorifying nor castigating them. But without the honor of being the nation's sacred starting point, early settlers seemed lacking.

For example, the nation's original heroes seemed to no longer possess that inventive turn of mind that the myth had showcased them possessing and that Frederick Jackson Turner had noted in his scholarly work. The president admitted that as the pioneers became "less primitive" they began to search for resources underground, albeit in a "rude manner." During President Washington's era, Roosevelt observed, "anthracite coal was known only as a useless black stone" while the "great fields of bituminous coal were undiscovered." He emphasized the early settlers' level of naiveté, as he believed that they possessed no inkling of steam power, used negligible amounts of water power, and used iron in "very small" ways. The nation's one-time frontier protagonists lacked too much knowledge to be crowned heroes of America's origin. "It is almost impossible for us in this day to realize how little our Revolutionary ancestors knew of the great store of natural resources," he mused, "and how little they required to take from this store in order to satisfy their needs."

Stretching the timeline backward positioned the pioneers as neither greedy nor corrupt, though. They simply followed an established historical trajectory. "From the first beginnings of civilization, on the banks of the Nile and the Euphrates," Roosevelt alleged, the "industrial progress of the world has gone on slowly, with occasional set-backs, but on the whole steadily." Even the Founding Fathers seemed to follow in lockstep as they created no great revolution in the nation's economic underpinnings: "When the founders of this nation met at Independence Hall . . . the conditions of commerce had not fundamentally changed from what they were when the Phoenician keels first furrowed the lonely waters of the Mediterranean." This steady and inexorable drive to build civilization that had influenced human activity for centuries removed the agency of pioneers. By removing their choice to act in a way different than their Phoenician forebears, Roosevelt altered their larger-than-life status to that of "average." Furthermore, he absolved them and, by extension, their successors, from receiving a moral judgment related to their abuse of the environment.

Roosevelt made a major revision to early American pioneers to allow for the conference's participants to be included and heralded in his version of a new mythic narrative. The former still represented strong and hard-working agents, but they failed to exhibit the value of foresight. While natural resource use by their ancestors had been minimal, the advances of people and industries since their arrival to North America had taken their toll. Stated another way, the scenic background for the protagonists—both old and new—had changed dramatically.

REMAKING MYTH: THE SCENE

The steady human activity on the historical timeline provided the rationale for Roosevelt's assessment of the current state of the union. He stated a simple, yet paradoxical idea. As people used the environment, they demanded more of it and simultaneously seemed to lose their sense of "dependence" upon it. This referred back to the Senate chaplain's benediction when he warned that people who used resources tended to forget from whence they came. That amnesia contributed to the overuse of resources.

Roosevelt noted that the rise of cities and industries separated the "average man" from his "close touch with nature" and thus, unknowingly, he failed to "realize the demands he is making upon nature." The president offered no pernicious reasoning for what was happening. He avoided the moral discussion of greed and other immoralities that had been a staple in his earlier addresses and that had riled his opponents. But he returned to arguments that he had been making for the last several years regarding the state of the environment. Knowledge, or rather the lack thereof, prevented a clear understanding that natural resources were being squandered. "This Nation began with the belief that its landed possessions were illimitable," Roosevelt declared, "and capable of supporting all the people who might care to make our country a home." But the fact that the "natural resources of the country are in danger of exhaustion" stemmed for the "old wasteful methods" used to acquire them. The president placed the blame on "old" ways of resource gathering, not the rapaciousness of industry barons or speculators—antiquated techniques, not people, appeared responsible. Without having to be defensive because of Roosevelt's usual castigations, the audience of business leaders could thus appreciate the extent of the problem in the current scene, and perhaps see the president as a leader and not a demagogue.

Roosevelt wanted to ensure that his audience recognized the problem as severe. This would be particularly difficult given the centuries-long belief in the infiniteness of natural resources, and with people's general unconcern with the future. Paul Cutright noted that at the turn of the twentieth century, concern about regulating environmental use to ensure adequate resources in the future was nonexistent. According to him, that "prevailing attitude" could be summed up by a question one congressman posed in response to him being asked to support conservation for the sake of posterity, "What has posterity ever done for me?"[47] Roosevelt needed to make the conference attendees afraid of what might happen if use of the environment went unchecked. Or, as Aristotle noted, people feel fear when "pain or destruction . . . appear to be not far off but near at hand and threatening."[48] The president worked to make the pain of posterity exist in the present day of the attendees.

To do that, Roosevelt employed the notion of "presence"—an argumentative technique that allows the audience to see and feel something that is not directly within its perception. One method involves a repetitious cataloguing of related data.[49] In a series of parallel statements, the president highlighted the urgency of the scene: "We began with an unapproached heritage of forests; more than half of the timber is gone. We began with coal fields more extensive than those of any other nation and with iron ores regarded as inexhaustible, and many experts now declare that the end of both iron and coal is in sight. . . . [We] began with soils of unexampled fertility, and we have so impoverished them by injudicious use . . . that their crop-producing power is diminishing." Unlike his stretching of time when discussing the mythic protagonists' altered status, the president now collapsed time between each event to bring more immediacy to the stark differences between the present scene and the past one. The phrase "we began" in the first clause of his statements further conditioned the audience to accept the implicit end that the latter clause was forecasting.

Roosevelt continued to manipulate time within the scene. He collapsed the timeline even further, moving the starting and endpoints within several decades of one another. "The mere increase in our consumption of coal during 1907 over 1906," he warned, "exceeded the total consumption in 1876." In other words, within the typical lifetime of the conference participants, they had witnessed "enormous stores of mineral oil and gas" depleted. Roosevelt even offered proof of the timeline by pointing to spokespeople who could confirm its validity. He asked that his guests speak to "those Governors who have in their State cities built up by natural gas, where the natural gas has been exhausted"—they would confirm the existing, dire status that the president alleged. Perhaps even more important, the shorter timeline introduced the threat to near-future generations. The careless use of resources in such a short period of time threatened the "prosperity of our children and children's children." The president connected the nebulous notion of posterity to the tangible offspring of the attendees. If the attendees acted too slowly for their own sake in this shortened timeline, they still possessed the opportunity to act for their children.

According to Roosevelt, America's future was now. For him, time collapsed into a single moment, one that saw the country achieve material greatness by the "rapid destruction" of nature. "[The] time has come to inquire seriously what will happen," he warned, offering a litany of problems that brought a chilling finality to the current scene, "when our forests are gone, when the coal, the iron, the oils, and the gas are exhausted, when the soils shall have been further impoverished and washed into the streams, polluting the rivers, denuding the field, and obstructing navigation. These questions do not relate only to the next century or to the next generation." The president clearly brought the myth's scenic problem to the present. That change, along with the modifications to the traditional protagonists, opened a space for the policies that would be needed to address the newly understood scene.

REMAKING MYTH: POLICY RECOMMENDATIONS

America's myth of origin—the Frontier Myth—represents one of the key "building blocks" in the nation's identity of divine inspiration and Americans' belief that they embody the greatest democratic culture in existence.[50] Early pioneers embraced that identity by conquering their infinite environment physically and economically. Eventually, legislators—either through ignorance or with intent—abetted business interests in their profitable destruction of nature. The assault on the environment, ironically, stemmed directly from the circular logic of the Frontier Myth, as it blessed any action America took because the country had been chosen by God to fulfill its destiny. Thus, Americans warred unmercifully against natives, as well as nature, because whatever the new nation did could be couched as a divine mandate.

In order to reconfigure the old myth and create a new storyline conducive to conservation, Roosevelt retold the Frontier Myth and revealed a story that designated pioneers as "average," and a scene that contained natural resources facing the "threat of imminent exhaustion." Slotkin noted that when "radical alterations" are made to heroic protagonists and the universal scene in which they exist, such as the ones the president had made, a new myth—a "new epoch of cultural history"—emerges.[51] With the old protagonists and scene now diminished in stature and replaced with new actors and a wildly revised universe, the president's storyline provided the guidance and the policies to fix the "reckless and wasteful use" perpetrated for centuries under the traditional myth.

Specifically, Roosevelt called for what he considered "wise use" of the environment, and coordination between invested parties to institute that wisdom, as the realization of the nation's democratic destiny. For him, policies that fostered "wise use" of the environment involved measures that reflected the practical realities of the scene—the national government overseeing conservation efforts that required national attention.

Roosevelt again distanced himself from preservationists by eschewing morality as the basis for change. He even poked fun at himself when he stated that the rapidity of the nation's "material growth" had not been matched by "spiritual and moral growth." The transcript for the speech indicated that he received "laughter and applause" when he admitted that "spiritual and moral growth" was "not the subject upon which I speak to you today." Instead of morality, the maintenance of the nation would come from the real-world expression of "energy and intelligence" of those attending. In other words, he offered foresight as the guiding value for decision-making. People with this sort of commonsense tendency did not replace those who brought technical expertise to bear, nor did they completely dismiss those interested in otherworldly reasons for safeguarding the environment; rather, it confirmed for attendees that they all had the potential wherewithal to embrace conservation. Roosevelt made the reality of the situation very simple. Either the attendees could continue to embrace the "average" primitiveness of their forebears, or they could demonstrate the single "distinguishing characteristic of really civilized men . . . foresight."

For Roosevelt, foresight began with "wise use" of the environment to foster homeownership. In this regard, the president hearkened back to what Henry Nash Smith labeled the "Jeffersonian ideal of a society of small landowners tilling their own soil."[52] This mythical frontier, and the desire of newcomers to establish their homesteads, represented both a birthright and a legacy. Roosevelt noted that it was the "prudent man" who exercised "foresight in conserving and wisely using the property," which manifested the "assurance of well-being for himself and his children." He urged that "we want to see a man own his farm rather than rent it, because we want to see it an object to him to transfer it in better order to his children. We want to see him exercise forethought for the next generation." The simple repetition of "we want" pulled the attendees together into a cooperative unit that supported the longevity of the culture, submerging any individual concerns about land use and land supervision in the process.

Even though the scene had changed due to centuries of wasting resources, the president alleged that awareness of this modest fact could begin to turn the situation around. "On the average the son of the farmer of today must make his living on his father's farm," and there was "no difficulty in doing this if the father will exercise wisdom. No wise use of a farm exhausts its fertility." By focusing on the homesteader and his family, Roosevelt avoided any discussions about unscrupulous land deals and predatory speculation that had allowed for the near-exhaustion of land resources. Although the president had recast the early settlers as "average," his use of the family home as part of the current policy connected present-day audiences with that romanticized element of family in the traditional myth.

Roosevelt's policy of foresight coupled with intelligent use set a standard for conserving the environment. It transcended the confusing and contradictory complex of state regulations for a variety of resources with a practicality that addressed those resources' longevity. His policy standard first simplified the natural world by dividing it "into two sharply distinguished classes" based on the opportunity for a resource's renewability. "In dealing with the coal, the oil, the gas, the iron, the metals generally," all needed to be "wisely used" as they will inevitably be exhausted. Here Roosevelt defined "wise use" as more than just common sense. Wise use depended on the "extraordinarily inventive genius of our people to devise means and methods for more or less adequately replacing what is lost." The second class of resources involved those that could "be improved by wise use . . . soil, the forest, the waterways. . . . [In] dealing with the soil and its products man can improve on nature by compelling the resources to renew." For example, he noted, "We can add enormous tracks of the most valuable possible agricultural land to the national domain by irrigation . . . and drainage of great tracts of swamp land. . . . . We can enormously increase our transportation facilities by the canalization of our rivers so as to complete a great system of waterways. . . ." Here again Roosevelt highlighted the farmer, or rather the agricultural expertise farmers needed to have, in order to fulfill their legacies to the next generation. More important, perhaps, he reiterated the idea of the interconnectedness of the environment. Revitalizing one element of nature, such as forests, could impact waterways, which could create more arable land. Ultimately, a comprehensive plan to use the environment wisely could appease industry leaders since the plan's outcome would result in the possibility of greater profits.

Support for a comprehensive plan that addressed the "wise use" and renewal of natural resources advanced another of Roosevelt's aims—the supervision of conservation efforts by the federal government. Dealing with the environment was beyond the control of any one state, as the president prudently envisioned a waterway system that extended from the "Pacific, Atlantic, and Gulf coasts and in the Mississippi Valley, from the Great Plains to the Alleghenies, and from the northern lakes to the mouth of the mighty Father of Waters." The interconnected nature of these resources called for "one coherent plan," not a "haphazard and piecemeal" one. Individual legislators thus found themselves constrained: Any decision they made after the conference had to reflect conserving nature through "inventive genius" to reflect the widest scope and largest benefit. Practically speaking, that meant their subservience to the coordination efforts that could only be overseen by the federal government, an organization that had already embraced the values of foresight and practicality.

Roosevelt confirmed this truth when he noted that he had "appointed the Waterways Commission" a year ago; he and that group had spent that time developing a coordinated policy to save the environment. In fact, he chided Congress that he had to "prosecute the work" by himself as he reminded the legislative body that it had refused the funds he wanted for the commission to operate.

Roosevelt's next act reflected what Tulis considered the epitome of the rhetorical presidency—Roosevelt publicly went over the heads of Congress to force it to accede to his request. The president declared, "I have asked Congress to pass a bill giving some small sum of money for the perpetuation of the [Waterways] Commission. If Congress does not act, I will perpetuate the Commission anyway, but of course it is a great deal better that Congress should act. . . . I hope there will be action. But the Commission will go ahead." The speech's transcript indicated "great applause" for Roosevelt's statement of undeterred activism despite congressional obstinacy. In fact, Roosevelt biographer Edmund Morris observed that the president's statement "won him his loudest ovation."[53] Roosevelt's challenge strategically positioned Congress on the "primitive" and "average" side of American culture by its initial refusal to fund the Inland Waterways Commission; it had seemingly dismissed the importance of foresight and thus rejected the practicality of "wise use." His rebuke appeared mild, however, given his years of blistering rhetoric directed at legislators he considered venal or incompetent.

After Roosevelt challenged Congress to act or else he would, he paused momentarily to recognize two key conference attendees. His recognition previewed the tradition contemporary presidents would employ during their State of the Union speeches: they identified particular citizens in the congressional gallery for public recognition as a means to embody their agendas.[54] Roosevelt first thanked the members of the Inland Waterways Commission. According to him, their "great personal sacrifice of time and effort" had "rendered a service to the public for which we can not be too grateful." The president reserved his most enthusiastic congratulations for the Bureau of Forestry chief. "Especial credit is due to the initiative, the energy, the devotion to duty, and the farsightedness of Gifford Pinchot, to whom we owe so much of the progress we have already made in handling this matter of the coordination and conservation of natural resources." The speech transcript noted that at the mention of Pinchot's name, the attendees erupted with "great applause." Roosevelt employed a tactic that would be made common by Ronald Reagan and his successors during their annual reports on the country's status.[55] By pointing to a living incarnation of a policy, accompanied by a thunderous ovation for that person, the president orchestrated a public confirmation of the policy's viability and worth by friends and foes alike. Pinchot had adopted the values that the president had been promoting, foresight and cooperation with government, as Roosevelt announced that, "If it had not been for him this convention neither would nor could have been called."

Roosevelt's insistence on what he described as "foresight" and "wise use" may have represented the greatest modification he made to the heart of the Frontier Myth. That traditional myth had struck an uneasy balance between the desires of the lone frontiersman and the desires of his community. As Janice Rushing observed, America's frontier protagonists faced a "dialectical tension" between the values they embraced. To be considered American, early settlers needed to "manifest rugged individualism" while responding "to the needs of a community."[56]

Roosevelt declared that that "dialectical tension" had swung out of balance and privileged the rugged individualist at the expense of the public. "We are coming to recognize as never before," he stated, "the right of the Nation to guard its own future in the essential matter of natural resources. In the past we have admitted the right of the individual to injure the future of the Republic for his own present profit. In fact there has been a good deal of a demand for unrestricted individualism, for the right of the individual to injure the future of all of us for his own temporary and immediate profit." The pendulum would now swing the other way.

With the president's elevation of "foresight" and "wise use" in the trajectory of his mythic narrative about the nation's frontier origin, he clearly dismissed the right of the rugged individual to misuse the environment now (albeit a misuse caused from lack of knowledge rather than from greed as had been Roosevelt's previous mantra). The past had been dominated by "primitive" thinking—individualism run rampant. Now was the time to embrace the lessons the reconfigured myth revealed: forethought and planned use of the environment would help "to protect ourselves and our children against the wasteful development of our natural resources, whether that waste is caused by the actual destruction of such resources or by making them impossible of development hereafter." Since that extreme individualism had been manifested by business leaders and their collaborators in Congress, the president positioned the executive branch as the only hope to rectify this cultural trend of environmental abuse with policies originating from government-sponsored units, such as the Inland Waterways Commission and the Bureau of Forestry.

Embracing "foresight" and "wise use" and their subsequent policies bypassed high-sounding morality—it involved soundness of mind and practicality. The president observed that "Any right thinking father earnestly desires and strives to leave his son both an untarnished name and a reasonable equipment for the struggle of life." Conservation did not guarantee material wealth; successive generations could only expect a continued "struggle," which was a hallmark of the nation's frontier origin. But it ensured that "right thinking" now would lead to a legacy that could "leave to the next generation the national honor unstained and the national resources unexhausted." For Roosevelt, simple survival was not enough. He wanted that survival, ensured by "resources unexhausted," to reflect a larger purpose. Individuals, such as the "right thinking father," needed to act in a way that protected his family, his nation, and affirmed the American democratic creed.

Roosevelt called on the final branch of government to sanction the values of "foresight" and "wise use" identified in the conversation between the executive and legislative branches. According to him, Maine's Supreme Court rendered a decision recently that made it clear that the judicial branch approved the "realization of this great truth" regarding national government supervision:

> "This opinion was rendered in response to questions as to the right of the Legislature to restrict the cutting of trees on private land for the prevention of droughts and floods, the preservation of the natural water supply, and the prevention of the erosion of such lands. . . . [A] policy of conservation . . . will preserve soil, forests, water power as a heritage for the children and the children's children of the men and women of this generation; for any enactment that provides for the wise utilization of the forests . . . and for the conservation of the water resources . . . must necessarily be legislation that will promote both private and public welfare. . . ."

The court's decision helped Roosevelt substantiate his position in several ways. It affirmed the government's right to control public land as it served to benefit the nation's wellbeing. Likewise, it diminished the mythic nature of the rugged individual and his right to do as he pleased. Roosevelt emphasized that when he avowed that the "opinion of the Maine Supreme

Bench sets forth unequivocally the principle that the property rights of the individual are subordinate to the rights of the community." The traditional myth kept individualism and community in tension with one another; what Roosevelt advocated in his retelling of the myth was the release of that tension, and the court confirmed it.

Conservation represented the management of resource use so that the country's wealth could pass down to future generations; it did not involve some starry-eyed, transcendentalist wish to keep the environment from being used, nor did it privilege the greedy capitalist who overused nature for profit. Furthermore, the court's decision elevated Pinchot's worth as its rendering positioned forests as the key to conservation writ large. As the chief forester, attendees needed to look to him to create policies and to supervise plans related to the interconnected elements of the environment.

Perhaps anticipating objections about state and national governments having the power to restrict resource use from business leaders, many of whom were in attendance in the East Room, the president explained how a policy of governmental supervision of nature did not prevent individuals from making money. He offered his policy interpretation of land ownership as his example.

Roosevelt charged that the Maine law affirmed the public's right to "control and limit the use of private property" through its government agent. He alleged that the state-owned land, as land itself, was "not the result of productive labor." According to him, land, in and of itself, was not worth anything until it was used. This was not a revolutionary idea. Considering that the federal government, under the Swamp Land Acts in the mid-nineteenth century, gave away land to several states for them to make that land profitable, Roosevelt's point seemed justified. Thus, the national government intended for the land it owned, as the public's representative, to be transferred to private owners, subsequently used, and to be made valuable. The states simply ensured that the land's profitability would not be wasted by individual owners who might clear-cut forests, for example.

According to Roosevelt, the Maine legislation did not authorize the state to "take private property"—the Constitution prohibited the execution of that law in that way. The worst corporate leaders could expect was a brief interruption in their traditional business processes. The law "might restrict the owner of wild and uncultivated lands in his use of them," Roosevelt assured his guests, it "might delay his taking some of the product, might delay his anticipated profits and thereby cause him some loss of profit," but it "would nevertheless leave him his lands, their product and increase, untouched, and without diminution of title, estate, or quantity. He would still have large measure of control and large opportunity to realize values." By accepting the law, industries that used natural resources would continue to reap their profits, practice the wisdom necessary to safeguard those resources through measured use, and uphold the community's importance over that of the individual. Or as the president summarized, a business leader "might suffer delay but not deprivation."

A typical Roosevelt strategy involved a binary choice that left audiences with little choice. "Delay" of expected profits and "wise use" of private land ownership proved much more agreeable policies than the alternative. Roosevelt subtly warned business leaders that things could be worse when he reaffirmed that the "proposed legislation would be within the legislative power and would not operate as a taking of private property for which compensation must be made." In highlighting the fact that the Maine legislation did not allow the government to take land from private owners, his statement still emphasized the government's ability to take privately owned land with other legislation that offered "compensation" when it did. The president even attempted to heighten the threat when he failed to mention anything about "fair" recompense if government felt the need to take privately owned land because of its owners' abuse of it. The business community would want to demonstrate foresight of its own and accept delay of its profits rather than risk outright seizure of them.

Roosevelt informed the audience that the Maine high court was not the only judicial body that had rendered a judgment in favor of conservation policies. The New Jersey Court of Errors and Appeals had echoed the Maine ruling in its own case. The defendant, the Hudson County Water Company, sued the state of New Jersey for breach of two contracts. The first contract gave the water company the right to pipe water to New York, while the second contract allowed the company to acquire that water from a New Jersey river. Responding for the state, the attorney general declared, "It shall be unlawful for any person or corporation to transport or carry . . . the waters of any fresh water . . . of this state into any other state" when the "health and prosperity of the citizens of New Jersey was at stake."[57] More important than that judgment, though, the nation's high court had "sustained" the New Jersey court ruling.

Roosevelt quoted at length the Supreme Court's decision, as written by Justice Oliver Holmes, which affirmed New Jersey's right to be responsible for safeguarding natural resources over any objection a private owner might have regarding the use of those resources.

> "It appears to us that few public interests are more obvious, indisputable and independent of particular theory than the interest of the public of a State to maintain the rivers that are wholly within it substantially undiminished, except by such drafts upon them as the guardian of the public welfare may permit for the purpose of turning them to a more perfect use."

Roosevelt could not have been more pleased with this ruling. The Supreme Court of the United States acknowledged that the government was the absolute and final arbiter in deciding issues related to using the environment. As expressed by Justice Holmes, the issue involved the practicality of leaving resources "substantially undiminished;" when the government did act to direct resource use, its action would presumably lead to "perfect use" of those resources in the public's interest, and not solely for private benefit.

The Supreme Court dismissed concerns corporations might have with theories of government related to the sanctity of private ownership, or prognostications private owners made about the potential loss of market value for resources no longer controlled by them. This part of the decision reflected the modern era angst that progressives sought to stem; this time the court sided with the "rudimentary wants" sought by the majority of citizens over the extravagant materialism pursued by lawyers for their business clients. In fact, Justice Holmes chided lawyers for their unfounded and myopic position, and drew laughter when Roosevelt read that part of the decision: "We are of opinion, further, that the constitutional power of the State to insist its natural advantages shall remain unimpaired by its citizen is not dependent upon any nice estimate of the extent of present use or speculation as to future needs. The legal conception of the necessary is apt to be confined to somewhat rudimentary wants, and there are benefits from a great river that might escape a lawyer's view." The government possessed the power to control natural resources without interference or "analysis" by non-governmental entities. This decision, the president concluded, reached the "root of the idea of conservation of our resources in the interest of our people."

With the Supreme Court ruling, Roosevelt's policy argument came full circle. The court agreed with the position that state governments, not private companies, had the legal right to make the only valid decisions regarding natural resources. But given the federal government's already demonstrated foresight and ability to organize efforts to address the interconnected nature of far-reaching environmental elements, it embodied the authorizing power as a key protagonist and overarching supervisor in the mythic narrative. The near-exhaustion of many natural resources in the current scene due to neglect of the public good deemed it necessary for federally-supervised/state-directed policies that ensured those resources be utilized wisely now, allowing those resources to be passed on to future generations.

Conservation, Roosevelt avowed, was only a prelude to a larger issue. For him, the premise of conservation related to the "problem of natural efficiency, the patriotic duty of insuring the safety and continuance of the Nation." He connected the controlled use of the environment to the "first of all the duties of true patriotism"—a citizen's obligation to work as hard as possible to achieve "excellence" across all facets of "national life." Conservation and patriotism, with both being national issues, fell to the federal government to promote. Acceptance of Roosevelt's new mythic storyline, then, ensured the "future of this Nation, in quality and in time." With those words, the transcript noted, attendees erupted in "great applause" and the morning session ended at 12:05 p.m.[58]

President Roosevelt's speech unveiled a new myth for modern America to embrace. Rather than blindly following the naiveté of their Puritan forbears that had led to the massive destruction of natural resources, the nation instead could embrace icons such as George Washington for their possession of the foresight required to assemble a country around the need for conservation. This new storyline absolved everyone involved for whatever moral or legal crimes they may have committed prior, affirmed the federal government's need to oversee conservation efforts across states, and called on legislators and industry leaders to work with the president in a spirit of collaboration. Roosevelt's speech set the stage for the rest of the conference to confirm his mythic storyline.

A CHORUS OF AGREEMENT

Although Roosevelt's speech ended, the Governors' Conference as a manifestation of his leadership continued. Attendees experienced the pomp and circumstance of this august affair as the president asked that attendees meet him, one by one, as they left the morning session, and for many to attend a dinner that evening. He maintained the majestic aura of a state event of the highest importance. Furthermore, the remaining session speakers for the next few days became spokespeople for the president's position. Even industry leaders who objected to what they considered the government's overreach regarding control of the environment appeared, at least superficially, as supporters given their participation in the conference. In an ironic twist of a rhetorical president who supposedly tries to usurp Congress's will by talking directly to the public, the conference positioned governors and business leaders to do Roosevelt's work for him and make the case for wise use and governmental oversight to an attentive public.

The afternoon session on day one of the conference saw millionaire Andrew Carnegie follow President Roosevelt to the podium. The steel tycoon served several purposes by immediately following the president. As one of the corporate elites routinely chastised by the president, his presence indicated that Roosevelt's narrative may have been a valid understanding of the nation's environmental problems, and thus scorned industry leaders like Carnegie were willing to work with him. Second, the steel magnate's choice as the second conference speaker perhaps showed the lineup was more than randomly decided: Of all the industry leaders, Carnegie had shown his support for Roosevelt years earlier by helping the president promote bird conservation; more than likely, the conference planners expected him to support Roosevelt now.[59]

Carnegie did just that. He applauded the active leadership of Roosevelt, likening him to George Washington. Both men made "good precedents," rather than simply follow them, Carnegie said, by each respectively calling their conferences to determine the best interests of the country. Just as Washington was known as the "father of the country," Carnegie afforded Roosevelt a similar distinction by naming him the first president's older son: "We are nationally in the position of a large family receiving a rich patrimony from thrifty parents deceased intestate; the President may be likened to the eldest son and the Governors to younger brothers." Not only was Roosevelt bestowed with Washington's authority as his direct descendant, his "elder son" status affirmed his power over the governors, described by Carnegie as his less mature siblings. In fact, Roosevelt's "far-sighted patriotism" outstripped anyone else in the room. According to the steel baron, the president embodied the daring of Thomas Jefferson pushing into unexplored territories, as well as the twin geniuses of Alexander Graham Bell and Thomas Edison, "kings among men" for "pushing into the unknown."

Beyond lavishing Roosevelt with extreme praise as a mythic and inventive hero, Carnegie echoed a key element of the president's narrative. Roosevelt claimed that ignorance, not avarice, explained contemporary environmental problems. Just as the president had softened his rhetoric against corporations for their greed, instead blaming lack of knowledge for the problems facing the nation, Carnegie followed suit. "It is staggering to learn," the steel mogul said about himself, "that our once-supposed ample supply of rich ores can hardly outlast the generation." Stated another way, Carnegie alleged that his fortune came not from unprincipled desires but from a cultural ignorance that the president's speech had already established. He reiterated Roosevelt's policy for "research" to guide the "control of national sources of material and power," which could extend the "career of prosperity."[60] Control, as executed by the states with federal government direction, Carnegie argued, meant use, and controlled use meant long-term profits.

The remaining speakers during the afternoon session of the first day reiterated much of the president's mythic narrative. They also broached issues that Roosevelt probably wanted left alone, such as the notion that corporate greed mandated government action, rather than federal oversight couched as a cooperative venture between newly informed partners. For example, I. C. White, the West Virginian state geologist, and John Mitchell, president of the United Mine Workers, painted a statistically-dismal picture of the scene: once abundant coal and oil resources now stood on the verge of depletion. Their warnings, though, also became a moral indictment of the business community, something Roosevelt avoided in his speech. "What will it profit this nation," White asked, "to have won the wreath of industrial supremacy, if in our thirst for gold and sudden riches we permit corporate greed . . . to waste and devastate the very sources of our prosperity? For just as sure as the sun shines and two and two is four, unless this insane riot of destruction and waste" is curbed, American civilization risked returning to a primitive age. Mitchell blamed the "mad rush for spoils and profits" for more than resource loss; it also accounted for the "criminal disregard of the personal safety and the lives of the men who toil in the mines. . . . Last year nearly 2,500 men were killed and more than 6,000 were seriously injured."

Roosevelt eschewed such condemnations, preferring instead to lay aside moral judgments to focus on lack of foresight, not greed, as the reason for current problems. His strategy assuaged corporate leaders' defensiveness and made them amenable to amendments to their ownership of resources, instead of offering attacks like White and Mitchell perpetrated.

The first day's closing speech undoubtedly heartened Roosevelt. University of Michigan President Dr. J. B. Angell reminded everyone of the "harmonious spirit" evident by the attendees, revealed that he cherished the "great pleasure" to be a part of such an unprecedented assemblage, and echoed Roosevelt's myth that the attendees stood equal to the gathering of men who framed the "Constitution of the United States." On that uplifting note, the first day of the conference ended at 5:05 p.m.[61]

The morning session on the second day began with a speech by another Roosevelt foe, James Hill, owner of the Great Northern Railroad. Large railroad companies had been notorious for their rate-fixing and stock manipulations.

In 1901, Hill forced a partnership between his operation and J. P. Morgan's Northern Pacific to create Northern Securities, a railroad monopoly deemed powerful enough to control the country. One of Roosevelt's first acts as president involved declaring war on Hill: he ordered the US Attorney General to sue Northern Securities under the Sherman Antitrust Act which eventually led the company to be dissolved. The clash with Hill highlighted Roosevelt's disdain of corporate wrongdoing and set the tone for the administration's reputation as a foe of corporate greed.[62]

Given their history, it seemed no surprise that Hill avoided thanking the president, unlike what most previous speakers did. But Hill sided with Roosevelt, stating again the belief that natural resources were now imperiled. He spoke at length about "soil waste," lamenting the fact that businesses had been "robbing the soil, in an effort to get the largest cash returns from each acre of ground in the shortest possible time and with the least labor." Such actions transformed America from a place with the "most fertile land in the world" into a country that "produces so much less than that of poorer quality elsewhere." Unlike White's and Mitchell's attacks on corporate interests, Hill's remarks perhaps resonated with his peers given his status as a tycoon. His indictment about corporate rapaciousness led him to repeat the solutions Roosevelt offered. He noted that the current environmental crisis required a nationwide awakening to "make men realize their duty toward coming generations exactly as the father feels it is a duty to see that his children do not suffer want." The "controlling policy" he called for was conservation, brought about by government-run scientific research, in order to sustain "material prosperity."[63] The fact that one of Roosevelt's chief antagonists echoed the president so closely sustained the validity of the latter's mythic narrative.

The remaining speakers during the morning session likewise repeated Roosevelt's argument about the interconnected nature of the environment, as well as affirmed the government's role in curbing resource waste for the public good. Lumber mogul R. A. Long called for forest conservation as a means to control soil erosion. Governor of New Jersey Franklin Fort urged waterway improvement to aid business development. Wisconsin Governor James Davidson noted that science and comprehensive legislation helped the state restore forested areas which in turn helped control flooding.[64]

The afternoon session of the second day, however, saw fireworks as some speakers turned against Roosevelt. The first speaker to do so came from the camp of preservationist thinkers, whose philosophy the president had already dismissed. J. Horace McFarland, president of the American Civic Association, granted the economic importance of natural resources, but called for the strict protection of those resources for aesthetic purposes. "Is the Grand Canyon of the Colorado," he asked, "to be really held as Nature's great temple of scenic color, or must we see that temple punctuated and profaned by trolley poles?" He answered decisively: civilization did not promote patriotism but scenic beauty did. He claimed that national parks, and areas such as Hetch Hetchy, needed to be "held absolutely inviolate." McFarland called out Roosevelt as a hypocrite for his apparent dismissal of the preservationists' position, scorning the president for the gall to take weekend visits "to his castle of rest in the Virginia Hills," and wondering why Roosevelt could not find "equal pleasure in Hoboken." In fact, the speaker charged the attendees as selfish, interested only in the "private beauty of scenery" for their own use. Despite the attack, Roosevelt benefitted as McFarland cast the president out of the preservationist camp, putting him on the side of like-minded businessmen who embraced "wise use" for maximum profits, and aiding Roosevelt's reimagining as a friend to industry. Unsurprisingly, when the speech ended, conference attendees chose not to applaud.[65]

Governor Edwin Norris of Montana challenged the president's use of the federal government to control state environments. He voiced particular concerns about the intentions of the Bureau of Forestry. For example, he pointed to a map that showed twenty-one million acres in Montana comprising national forests and called on the interior secretary to stop creating more forest reserves. Norris argued that the reasoning for more reserves did not apply in his state. Forest reserves that protected the soil were not needed since Montana "soil does not wash away;" nor were the reserves needed for lumber as that was not "of supreme importance" either. The governor rejected conservation efforts regarding crop production. "When I hear you gentlemen talk of producing ten or fifteen or twenty bushels of wheat per acre," he scolded, "I am moved to say that I should like to take you into the Judith basin in our State, where last year they produced sixty bushels of wheat to the acre, and were not specially vain of that yield either." Norris ended by questioning Roosevelt's right to keep the fees generated from ranchers using the federal range land in Montana. Applause erupted throughout Norris's speech.[66]

James Garfield, the secretary of the interior, pushed back on Governor Norris's closing question about which entity—state or federal government—deserved the revenue from use of a resource located in that state. Garfield responded with his own question: "Why should a great resource owned, as the Gentleman admits, by the People at large, be used by private interests, by somebody who is looking only to his own benefit, and not to the benefit of the People of the country?" Garfield chastised Norris, connecting him to the venal pursuits of private businesses in their use of natural resources, reminding everyone that the federal government collected those revenues to benefit the nation, not just private interests or state coffers. Implicitly, Garfield alluded to the decades-long corruption common between state legislatures and corporate interests that had decimated nature, thus promoting the federal government as the impartial arbiter of both environmental and monetary resources in the process. Garfield offered an olive branch to governors concerned with federal overreach, though. He repeatedly assured them that he sided with them when they objected to the federal government "attempting to overreach and come into their States for purposes not authorized by law." He declared that the very fact of this conference wiped away that erroneous belief. The conference asserted the right of the federal government to develop natural resources "for the greatest good to the greatest number which do not lie simply within one State," and demonstrated that it and the states stood together to prevent future misuse of the environment.

Although Garfield assigned moral blame, rather than a lack of foresight for current problems, he reiterated Roosevelt's position that federal authority was needed to save the nation. Like Norris's speech, Garfield's address drew several instances of applause.[67] The rest of the speakers in the afternoon session repeated the themes outlined in Roosevelt's address.

Before the morning session began on the conference's last day, the Committee on Resolutions presented its report. Days earlier, Roosevelt appointed several governors to form a committee to summarize the results of the proceedings and to make recommendations for future endeavors. Governor Blanchard of Louisiana read the committee's pronouncements into the record: He underscored the "high duty" necessary to ensure that conservation efforts would be utilized to prevent resource exhaustion; labeled conservation as a "subject of transcendent importance;" commended Roosevelt's "wise forethought" in alerting the nation to wasteful environmental practices and gathering the conference membership to "seek remedies;" called on each state to develop a commission that would cooperate with other state commissions regarding conservation efforts; and suggested that future conferences called by the president with similar guest lists be organized. Blanchard's concluding statement, "Let us conserve the foundations of our prosperity," generated "great applause" from the gathering, probably heartening business leaders with its linking of natural resources to wealth, and pleasing Roosevelt with its implicit call for "wise use" of the environment.

The Committee on Resolutions' "Declaration" communicated an air of formal acceptance. Its series of declarative statements about what was needed, the powers invested in various entities, and the general affirmation of the nation's wellbeing—all punctuated by applause—called forth the memory of the nation's founding document, which, according to Roosevelt and numerous others during the conference, had likewise been borne out of a similar gathering. Whether the members of the Committee on Resolutions realized it or not, their document's opening lines had mimicked the preamble of the Constitution:

Declaration	*Constitution*
"We, the Governors of the States and Territories of the United States of America, in Conference assembled, do hereby declare the conviction that the great prosperity of our country rests upon the abundant resources of the land chosen by our forefathers for their homes and where they laid the foundation of this great nation."	"We the People of the United States, in Order to form a more perfect Union, establish Justice, insure domestic Tranquility, provide for the common defence, promote the general Welfare, and secure the Blessings of Liberty to ourselves and our Posterity, do ordain and establish this Constitution for the United States of America."

The Governors' Conference attendees resembled the original "perfect union" who recognized natural resources as the key to promoting the "general Welfare," implying its "foundation" would establish a future—"Posterity"—reflecting the greatness of the nation.[68] Roosevelt's committee legitimized his revision of America's mythic origin involving conservationist goals by re-creating the nation's founding document at the conference.

After reading the Declaration, Governor Blanchard raised a point about an omission from the document. He noted that the Committee on Resolutions considered adding a statement about the states' governors having the ability to gather together on their own to discuss conservation without a presidential request, but chose to omit it. North Carolina's governor, Robert Glenn, made the motion to include that amendment and several governors voiced their support for it. Governor Joseph Folk of Missouri spurred gales of laughter and applause when he identified the governors' fear—that the president may refuse to gather the governors if they wanted to meet, and, perhaps more important, that the president might only call them together for his own political gain. "Suppose that some time in the future there should be a man" in the presidency, Folk wondered, "who would want to use such power or prestige as might be obtained from a gathering of the Governors to coerce Congress, for instance, into adopting some law. . . . So I for one am unwilling to commit . . . to what may possibly be used merely as an instrument to accomplish something with another branch of the Government." Folk's statement jabbed at Roosevelt's intentions for hosting this conference, as well as called into question the president's desire to manifest a rhetorical leadership that could unduly force Congress' hand. Governor Edmund Noel from Mississippi generated "laughter and applause" of his own when he admitted that he believed the purpose of this conference was for governors to "exercise moral suasion on our Senators and Representatives" to help their states' environmental conditions. With that blunt observation about what presidential leadership had wrought, Governor Glenn withdrew his motion.[69]

The most important speaker during this last session was William Jennings Bryan. Conference attendees probably expected the Democratic Party leader to blast his host's policies as he had plans to challenge Roosevelt's vice-president, William Howard Taft, in the 1908 presidential election (having already sought the presidency twice before). For the most part, he sided with Roosevelt. Bryan acknowledged that the conference marked the "beginning of a new era" in which nationwide attention would be given to the issue of conservation. Of particular note, he recognized the importance of the "epoch-making speech" that Roosevelt had delivered as the means to "exert a powerful influence upon the country at large, as it has upon those who were fortunate enough to hear him." He too communicated his concern for the unrestricted use of the nation's assets and considered who best might control that use. Calling himself a "strict constructionist," Bryan noted that he frowned on "encroachment on the rights of the States." But rather than oppose Roosevelt's promotion of the federal government's need to direct conservation policy, or object to the president's litany of executive orders, he offered a Solomon-like compromise. "It is just as imperative that the general Government shall discharge the duties delegated to it," he stated, "as it is that the States shall exercise powers reserved to them." Both entities, he believed, had found "communion together" at the conference and could work agreeably to foster investments in the environment now for realization in the future.[70]

The rest of the session followed form. The speakers—all governors, lieutenant governors, and other representatives filling in for a state's absent governor—echoed several of the conference themes. Nebraska Governor George Sheldon subordinated the states' rights to the federal government's power, calling for the latter to "assist . . . more than they have in the past." A. E. Mead, governor of Washington, noted that he had already begun working with the lumber industry to conserve dwindling forest reserves. Businessman William Louden, filling in for Iowa's governor, called conservation a "subject . . . of incalculable moment" now for generations to come. Following the passage of a resolution to include in the conference's written proceedings those presentations that were not made publicly, Roosevelt thanked the attendees, called them the most "distinguished" guests ever welcomed to the White House, and adjourned the conference.[71]

All of the formality, the majesty, the state-of-the-union like format, and Roosevelt's storyline marking a pivotal moment for the destiny of the country would have gone for naught if the mass media failed to tell the story once the proceedings ended. Thanks to Roosevelt's years of courting and coercing of the press, and the administration's inundation of conference minutiae months before the event, journalists heralded the event a huge success. For example, the *New-York Tribune* enthusiastically proclaimed that the president's speech exhibited his "characteristic vigor," which was appreciated by attendees who frequently interrupted his speech with applause.[72] *The Washington Times* echoed the president's foundational narrative plot point about the historical significance of the conference, labeling it as the "most important gathering of public men in the United States since the signing of the Declaration of Independence." That newspaper's headline, "President Cheered by the Governors," dismissed any conflict between Roosevelt and the state chief executives; its headline referred to the accompanying news story that the governors agreed with the president's position regarding the necessary use of federal power for conservation.[73] *The Washington Herald* presented the governors' subordination to the president in a more comical fashion. On its front page cartoon, a circle of governors, no taller than toddlers with the word "governors" spelled out across their backs, held hands as they danced around the imposing adult figure of Roosevelt, himself sporting a wry smile, with William Jennings Bryan looking on unamused.[74]

Roosevelt's rhetorical leadership—his speech and the attending conference—generated near-unanimous coverage. Pinchot's persistence with inundating newsrooms with information undoubtedly accounted for the similarity of wording across several different newspapers. For example, the *Los Angeles*

Herald, the *Daily Press*, and *The Salt Lake Herald* all carried verbatim copy to open their front page stories: "The first conference of the governors of the states of the American union ended today. . . . The printed record of the conference, which will later be available to every American home, will be a compilation of facts, startling in their meaning, convincing in their universal conclusion . . . that the states and the nation must cooperate . . . [so] that the whole people of the nation may accrue the lasting benefit of its natural resources."[75] Between Roosevelt's institutional gravitas and reinterpretation of America's mythic past during the conference, along with the meticulous planning of the event, the mass media trumpeted the president's wisdom and gentlemanly authority to lead the nation on matters of conservation.

Five

Roosevelt's Rhetorical Legacy

Despite Roosevelt using his rhetorical power to promote various aspects of conservation, his accomplishments regarding the Governors' Conference might appear, at first glance, checkered. For example, Samuel Hays concluded that the event proved futile. According to him, immediately following the conference, the president asked for Congress to fund the National Conservation Commission (NCC) and its work to inventory the country's natural resources. "Congress not only denied his request," Hays wrote, "but also approved the Tawney Amendment to the Sundry Civil Bill, prohibiting any federal administrative official from aiding the work of any executive commission not authored by Congress." This represented the legislators' line-in-the-sand to communicate to Roosevelt that he had exceeded his authority in "assuming legislative powers."[1]

While Congress's refusal perhaps reflected one measure of failure, another might involve President Taft—Roosevelt's hand-picked successor—who did not feel motivated to continue on with his predecessor's environmental activism. Even more egregious, Taft planned to alter conservation policy due to his doubt regarding the legality (in spirit if not the letter of the law) of some of Roosevelt's executive orders. Finally, President Taft quickly fired the previous president's high-ranking appointees involved in conservation—Secretary of the Interior James Garfield, and Roosevelt's good friend, Gifford Pinchot, chief of the US Forest Service.[2]

The "all or nothing" position of critics who decry the president's rhetorical ability to ensure immediate change, or who limit that ability only to one speech given, miss other effects. Congress denied funding the NCC but the organization still performed its herculean task of inventorying the nation's resources. Roosevelt's many public appearances and rhetorical leadership identified him as a vocal supporter for such administrative efforts, probably inspiring the NCC's membership to take on the task despite already having full-time jobs and no budget for their volunteer work. Moreover, Roosevelt's speech, and the rhetoric of the Governors' Conference event itself, spurred nearly all the states to create their own state-run commissions to address conservation efforts. Remember that the governors were so inspired during the conference to tackle environmental problems that they initially took umbrage with the belief that only the president could call them together to discuss conservation. That inspiration likely came from Roosevelt's cowboy persona and his unique retelling of the Frontier Myth, as biographer Patricia O'Toole remarked that the governors left the event "hell-bent on stopping crimes" against the environment like duly deputized "sheriffs."[3]

Roosevelt clearly demonstrated the effectiveness of presidential rhetorical performances. Going into the May 1908 event, critics identified the president as a tyrant who unabashedly used executive orders against congressional will and in defiance of business interests. He responded with the Governors' Conference, an event that Mary Stuckey might label as Roosevelt's attempt at "interpretative dominance." He used a revised myth of national origin to affirm the presidency as the rightful guardian of natural resources and enhanced the institutional power of that office; simultaneously, he appeased Congress and business interests by rhetorically constructing them as equal partners in the process of protecting the nation. By connecting himself and the Governors' Conference mythically and temporally to George Washington and that president's waterways conference, Roosevelt minimized the controversial nature of his previous actions. His linking of the presidency to the cultural values embodied in his new myth of America's origin helped to naturalize the act of a president attempting to enhance his institutional primacy.[4]

Roosevelt inspired action beyond the moment of his speech and the Governors' Conference itself. For example, even with Pinchot's ouster from the Taft administration, the conservationist stubbornly continued his friend's legacy. Borrowing a page from Roosevelt, Pinchot assembled a diverse cadre of alliances—newly enfranchised women voters and common male laborers—to propel him into the governorship of Pennsylvania for two terms, one in 1923 and the other eight years later. As governor, Pinchot sought to influence conservation policy at both state and national levels.[5]

President Roosevelt made the principles and policies of "wise use," "foresight," and "federal control" important in that moment at the conference and beyond. The May 16, 1908, edition of the *Bisbee Daily Review* summarized the long-term efficacy of the president's public rhetorical performance: "Like many important events in history, time will be needed to reveal the epoch which the president and governors believe has been made. The accomplishments of the conference . . . cannot be set forth with mathematical precision. That immediate result will be more than ample is the expression of President Roosevelt, who brought it about, and of the governors who participated."[6] That newspaper grasped the subtleties of what Roosevelt's rhetorical leadership had accomplished—it would take time to know exactly how much had been done, but the evidence of success was already apparent. Roosevelt's rhetorical performance had been successful because the conference had actually occurred, while likewise planting the seeds for future developments to take root. As biographer Paul Cutright observed, the "National Conservation Commission lived on until 1923. By that time hundreds of people were talking conservation for every one who had talked it when Roosevelt called the first general conservation conference in 1908."[7]

Roosevelt restored his persona as a respected chief executive because of his address and the rhetorical production that was the Governors' Conference. Despite *The Nation's* lengthy rebukes that the May event brought about no immediate change and provided "no Novum Organon [*sic*] of government to remove all our political ills," it still concluded that the president had been rhetorically effective. The magazine admitted:

> "It is praise enough for President Roosevelt that he has succeeded, by his recourse to a gathering of the Governors, in giving a new impetus to the study and settlement of important national questions. They will not appear again quite the same. He has given the country a new way of looking at these problems. When discussion arises hereafter, or laws are proposed, concerning the preservation and care of forests, soil, mines, waterways, those who oppose action or legislations will have to be more careful, as men who now know that a great body of educated opinion and political influence has been evoked in favor of checking the reckless and wanton exhaustion of the gifts with which nature has so richly endowed our land. For this, we all owe the President sincere acknowledgments. He has never appeared more statesmanlike than in looking anxiously to the physical future of the country; and in so easily and naturally obtaining the assistance of the Governors, Mr. Roosevelt has given the whole cause added momentum. That, we have no reason to doubt, was his sole object."[8]

Critics that limit the success of a "rhetorical presidency" to one narrowly defined, single speech misrepresent the power of rhetoric. Roosevelt demonstrated that a public speech act (broadly defined) falling under a comprehensive notion of the "rhetorical presidency" is no magic trick that occurs in the blink of an eye. Using discourse to shape and to move multiple constituencies represents a long-term process that requires an adept advocate like Roosevelt to recognize and to meet the intellectual, political, and social challenges facing him.

Those challenges were enormous. The president faced centuries of ingrained beliefs and cultural attitudes about the infinite nature of nature and the need to conquer it to stave off the supposed devils hiding in the environmental darkness. Roosevelt realized that natural resources represented a site for wealth, power, and corruption that seemed to resist change. He recognized the confounding sets of legislation that had to be negotiated with business and political interests in the public eye. The swirling intricacies of all these challenges made the safeguarding of nature appear insurmountable during Roosevelt's political career.

Yet Roosevelt took on the challenge astutely, adapting the well-established rhetorical nature of the presidency to fit and to guide the political and social elements of his era. He reaffirmed the presidency as an institution that needed to actively engage with the public. He turned the mass media to his use, providing colorful copy to it as his peripatetic actions took him from private residences to the scenic vistas of nature's cathedrals, giving his words about conserving the environment rapt and continuous audiences. He co-opted Washington traditions, such as those associated with the State of the Union, to borrow the majesty of them for his own institutional rehabilitation. That allowed him the forum to retell America's origin, lessening pioneer-based obstinacy in a way that situated Roosevelt, and his pragmatic plans for corporate buy-in to national government oversight, as the rightful legacy of the Founding Fathers.

Looking around today at various environmental concerns it may seem difficult to praise Roosevelt for his efforts more than a century ago. America and the world still seem to be at odds over the protection of nature, reliving the same issues that plagued the father of conservation. For example, issues of who has the right to dictate use of land continue to bedevil the federal government. In 2014, Nevada rancher Cliven Bundy refused to recognize the Bureau of Land Management's right to impose grazing fees, going so far as to engage in an armed standoff with local authorities to uphold what he believed his God-given right to use nature as he pleased.[9] The continued debate on the reality of climate change provides no solace from real-world effects. A deadly mudslide in a rural Seattle neighborhood in 2014, while unprecedented in its destructiveness, was not unforeseen as increased rainfall due to changes in the climate saturated an area already prone to landslides because of clear-cutting in nearby forested areas.[10] Unrestrained industrial activity has tainted air quality almost beyond repair. Scientists in China have warned that pollution in their country has now reached toxic levels and spurred people to buy face masks when venturing outside. The smoky haze of this "nuclear winter" even threatens their plant-based food supply.[11] Although Roosevelt's cherished buffalos made a comeback, other animals have not been so lucky. Unabated consumer demand for ivory makes even the most protected wildlife sites vulnerable to determined poachers who wantonly slaughter elephants—animals that now appear on the verge of extinction.[12]

Although dire concerns, the responses to them actually reveal Roosevelt's rhetorical legacy as environment issues do not go unchallenged by a disinterested public or political class. For example, media concluded that Bundy's defiance of federal authority, once seen as a legitimate reason to debate enforcement of land use, was nothing more than a "scofflaw disobeying a Court Order."[13] Despite failed government attempts to stop animal slaughter, another powerful entity took up the challenge in 2014. Social media blasted a college cheerleader known for her hunting and killing of rare big game such as elephants and rhinos. It successfully prevented her from posting pictures of her prizes on Facebook, essentially denouncing the act of big-game hunting as a means to test "manhood" (much to Roosevelt's chagrin if he were alive).[14]

Contemporary media also reported that President Obama planned for federal leadership on climate change. In the process it unknowingly positioned Obama as an heir to President Roosevelt, as Obama also engaged in both collaborative and cowboy approaches to current environmental problems. When Obama announced a move to reduce emissions from power plants and make America a leader by example, one journalist echoed his brethren from Roosevelt's time, marveling, "We finally have a president that understands science. We finally have a president that honestly includes scientists as decision makers—rather than effectively muzzle them. We finally have a president that recognizes the social and economic costs of climate change. . . . Can you imagine, a President of the US with a well-publicized effort to articulate the importance of climate change and the need for action? It's the dawn of a new day."[15] Roosevelt understood the science and sought cooperation but was willing to go it alone. So too did Obama. Obama announced that he would bypass Congress and invoke the Antiquities Act to "create the world's largest marine reserve in the Pacific, banning fishing and other commercial activities across vast swaths of pristine sea populated by whales, dolphins, and sea turtles and dotted with coral atolls." According to one source, the use of the Antiquities Act on such a "sheer scale" cemented "Obama's conservation legacy."[16]

Quite the contrary to critics of Roosevelt's discourse not instantaneously transforming the political landscape, nor effecting long-lasting changes to the nation's awareness and will, he used the rhetorical nature of the presidency in a revolutionary way for his time. He helped to establish a new way of thinking about the environment—and the president's responsibility for it—by creating an event unique in America history. His speech at the Governors' Conference, and the majesty of the event itself, utilized the tools at hand—the media to trumpet a message of pragmatic collaboration for future generations, buoyed by empowering traditions of myth and presidential speaking—to provide momentum to an idea that has not yet lost its energy. As Harbaugh noted in 1963 about Roosevelt's long shadow over conservation:

> "If, a half century later, many state governments stand paralyzed before the special interest that Roosevelt fought; if, thirty years after Roosevelt's death, private power companies continue to build dams without regard for the multi-purposes he urged; if, only rarely, a governor emerges with the courage and the vision to rise above the short-sighted economy that Roosevelt deplored; if all this in our times is true, it is also true that the very substantial achievements of the past fifty years reflect the animating spirit of Theodore Roosevelt."[17]

The only correction to be made to Harbaugh's observation about Roosevelt's "spirit" is that it continues to animate us today.

Notes

CHAPTER ONE

1. Theodore Roosevelt, *An Autobiography* (New York: Charles Scribner's Sons, 1929), 395.

2. Roderick F. Nash, *Wilderness and the American Mind,* 4th ed. (New Haven: Yale University Press, 2001), 102–104; Samuel P. Hays, *Conservation and the Gospel of Efficiency: The Progressive Conservation Movement, 1890–1920* (Pittsburgh: University of Pittsburgh Press, 1999), ix–xii.

3. For the observation on laissez faire, see Doris Kearns Goodwin, *The Bully Pulpit: Theodore Roosevelt, William Howard Taft, and the Golden Age of Journalism* (New York: Simon & Schuster, 2013), xi; for the quoted material, see Timothy Egan, *The Big Burn: Teddy Roosevelt and the Fire That Saved America* (Boston: Mariner Books, 2009), 49.

4. William H. Harbaugh, *The Life and Times of Theodore Roosevelt* (New York: Collier Books, 1963), 311; Douglas Brinkley, *The Wilderness Warrior: Theodore Roosevelt and the Crusade for America* (New York: Harper Perennial, 2009), 795.

5. See Roosevelt, *An Autobiography,* 420–422; Brinkley, *The Wilderness Warrior*, 825–828.

6. Beth Taylor-Park Ranger, "Inside Yellowstone-Roosevelt Arch," National Park Service online video, April 27, 2007, http://www.nps.gov/media/video/view.htm?id=242E3EA9–155D-451F-675B40BB539D6424; Martin Miller, "Roughing it at Yellowstone's Roosevelt Lodge," *Los Angeles Times*, July 26, 2010, http://articles.latimes.com/2010/jul/26/travel/la-tr-roosevelt-20100725.

7. "Theodore Roosevelt and Conservation," National Park Service, http://www.nps.gov/thro/historyculture/theodore-roosevelt-and-conservation.htm.

8. For example, see Elizabeth Palermo, "Unhappy Feet: Emperor Penguins Threatened by Climate Change," *CBS News* video, July 1, 2014, http://www.cbsnews.com/news/unhappy-feet-emperor-penguins-threatened-by-climate-change/; "Conservation Celebrity Campaigners & Charities," Look To the Stars: The World of Celebrity Giving, accessed May 15, 2015, https://www.looktothestars.org/cause/conservation; Doug Horn, "Record Number of Visitors for Glacier National Park in Montana," *Design & Trend,* September 9, 2014, http://www.designntrend.com/articles/19234/20140909/visitors-glacier-national-park-montana.htm; "George H. W. Bush Domestic Politics," *PBS: American Experience*, accessed May 15, 2015, http://www.pbs.org/wgbh/americanexperience/features/general-article/bush-domestic/; Barack Obama, "President Obama Designates Five New National Monuments," The White House, March 25, 2013, https://www.whitehouse.gov/the-press-office/2013/03/25/president-obama-designates-five-new-national-monuments; Joe Galli, "My Republic Rewards Program Entices Community to Recycle," *NBC24.com*, August 14, 2011, http://www.nbc24.com/news/story.aspx?id=655192#.VBB0cPldV8E; Ken Ritter, "Hillary Clinton: US Should Lead on Clean Energy," *The Washington Times*, September 5, 2014,http://www.washingtontimes.com/news/2014/sep/5/hillary-clinton-us-should-lead-clean-energy/?page=all.

9. Frank E. Smith, *The Politics of Conservation* (New York: Pantheon Books, 1966), 108.

10. Hays, *Conservation and the Gospel of Efficiency*, 140.

11. Jeffrey K. Tulis, *The Rhetorical Presidency* (Princeton: Princeton University Press, 1987), 114. Roosevelt's use of the "rhetorical presidency" will be covered at length in Chapter 3.

12. Gary L. Gregg II, *The Presidential Republic: Executive Representation and Deliberative Democracy* (Lanham: Rowman & Littlefield Publishers, Inc., 1997), 138.

13. Samuel Kernell, *Going Public: News Strategies of Presidential Leadership*, 3rd ed. (Washington, D. C.: Congressional Quarterly Inc., 1997), 74–75.

14. George C. Edwards III, *On Deaf Ears: The Limits of the Bully Pulpit* (New Haven: Yale University Press, 2003), ix, 241.

15. David Zarefsky, "The Presidency Has Always Been a Place for Rhetorical Leadership," in *The Presidency and Rhetorical Leadership*, ed. Leroy G. Dorsey, (College Station: Texas A&M University Press, 2002), 20–41; Stephen E. Lucas, "George Washington and the Rhetoric of Presidential Leadership," in *The Presidency and Rhetorical Leadership*, 42–72.

16. Martin J. Medhurst, "Was There a Nineteenth-Century Rhetorical Presidency? A Debate Revisited," in *Before the Rhetorical Presidency*, ed. Martin J. Medhurst, (College Station: Texas A&M University Press, 2008), 2–3. Medhurst makes a distinction between the "rhetorical presidency" and "presidential rhetoric" in the edited collection, *Beyond the Rhetorical Presidency* (College Station: Texas A&M University, 1996), xi–xxv. For purposes of this book, I will sometimes subsume those terms within the notion of "rhetorical leadership;" See Leroy G. Dorsey, "Introduction: The President as a Rhetorical Leader," in *The Presidency and Rhetorical Leadership*, 3–19. My point here is that the president's rhetorical leadership, whether at an institutional level or not, identifies a much broader definition of rhetoric use, one that reflects what Medhurst labeled "rhetorical being"—a person (president) who takes the complexities of context and audience into account to construct discourse that assists others to navigate the "vicissitudes of human existence." See Martin J. Medhurst, "Afterword: The Ways of Rhetoric," in *Beyond the Rhetorical Presidency*, ed. Martin J. Medhurst, ed. (College Station: Texas A&M University Press, 1996), xi–xii, 219.

17. For examples, see Barry Brummett, *Reading Rhetorical Theory* (Fort Worth: Harcourt College Publishers, 2000); Sonja K. Foss, Karen A. Foss, and Robert Trapp, *Contemporary Perspectives on Rhetoric*, 30th Anniversary Ed. (Long Grove: Waveland Press, 2014).

18. Kenneth Burke, *A Rhetoric of Motives* (New York: Prentice-Hall, Inc., 1952), 41–44.

19. Kathleen H. Jamieson, *Eloquence in an Electronic Age: The Transformation of Political Speechmaking* (New York: Oxford University Press, 1988), 180.

20. Mary Stuckey, "Establishing the Rhetorical Presidency through Presidential Rhetoric: Theodore Roosevelt and the Brownsville Raid," *Quarterly Journal of Speech* 92.3 (2006), 289, 302.

21. See H. W. Brands, *T.R.: The Last Romantic* (New York: Basic Books, 1997), 624–625; Edmund Morris, *Theodore Rex* (New York: Random House, 2001), 496–519; Goodwin, *The Bully Pulpit*; Paul R. Cutright, *Theodore Roosevelt: The Making of a Conservationist* (Urbana: University of Illinois Press, 1985), 228–230; Paul R. Cutright, *Theodore Roosevelt: The Naturalist* (New York: Harper & Brothers, 1956), 180–183; Brinkley, *The Wilderness Warrior*, 770–773. For other historical sources that deal with some aspect of Roosevelt's speech, see J. Leonard Bates, "Fulfilling American Democracy: The Conservation Movement, 1907 to 1921," *The Mississippi Valley Historical Review* 44.1 (1957): 29–57; Stephen Ponder, "'Publicity in the Interest of the People': Theodore Roosevelt's Conservation Crusade," *Presidential Studies Quarterly* 20.3 (1990): 547–555.

22. James B. White, *When Words Lose Their Meaning: Constitutions and Reconstitutions of Language, Character, and Community* (Chicago: The University of Chicago Press, 1984), xi.

23. Leroy G. Dorsey, "The Frontier Myth in Presidential Rhetoric: Theodore Roosevelt's

Campaign for Conservation," *Western Journal of Communication* 59 (1995): 1–19; Leroy G. Dorsey, "Preaching Conservation: Theodore Roosevelt and the Rhetoric of Civil Religion," in *Green Talk in the White House*, ed. Tarla R. Peterson (College Station: Texas A&M University Press, 2004), 40; Leroy G. Dorsey, "Theodore Roosevelt and the Progressive Impulses of Conservation," in *Green Voices: Defending Nature and the Environment in American Civic Discourse*, eds. Richard D. Besel and Bernard K. Duffy (Albany: State University of New York Press), forthcoming.

24. Daniel O. Buehler, "Permanence and Change in Theodore Roosevelt's Conservation Jeremiad," *Western Journal of Communication* 62.4 (1998): 441, 452–453, 455.

25. Jessica Sheffield, "Theodore Roosevelt, 'Conservation as a National Duty,'" *Voices of Democracy* 5 (2010): 89, 98.

26. David Barry, *Forty Years in Washington* (1924; repr., New York: Beekman Publishers Inc., 1974), 275.

27. Brinkley, *The Wilderness Warrior*, 759–765.

28. Egan, *The Big Burn*, 42.

29. Richard T. Hughes, *Myths America Lives By* (Urbana: University of Illinois Press, 2003), 2, 19, 28.

30. Kenneth Burke, "Revolutionary Symbolism in America," in *The Legacy of Kenneth Burke*, eds. Herbert W. Simons and Trevor Melia (Madison: University of Wisconsin Press, 1989), 267; Claude Levi-Strauss, *The Savage Mind* (Chicago: The University of Chicago Press, 1966), 16. The literature on myths suffusing American culture is extensive, but for other representative examples, see James O. Robertson, *American Myth, American Reality* (New York: Hill & Wang, 1980); Brian W. Dippie, *Custer's Last Stand: The Anatomy of an American Myth* (Lincoln: University of Nebraska Press, 1976); Henry N. Smith, *Virgin Land: The American West as Symbol and Myth* (Cambridge: Harvard University Press, 1978); Greg Dickinson, Brian L. Ott, and Eric Aoki, "Memory and Myth at the Buffalo Bill Museum," *Western Journal of Communication* 69.2 (2005), 85–108; Phillip J. Chidester, "'The Toy Store of Life': Myth, Sport and the Mediated Reconstruction of the American Hero in the Shadow of the September 11th Terrorist Attacks," *Southern Communication Journal* 74.4 (2009): 352–372; Janice H. Rushing, "The Rhetoric of the American Western Myth," Communication Monographs 50.1 (1983): 14–32.

31. Roland Barthes, *Mythologies*, trans. Annette Lavers (New York: The Noonday Press, 1972), 143.

CHAPTER TWO

1. John Opie, *Nature's Nation: An Environmental History of the United States* (Fort Worth: Harcourt Brace College Publishers, 1998), 15–17.

2. Alan Taylor, "'Wasty Ways': Stories of American Settlement," in *American Environmental History*, ed. Louis S. Warren (Malden: Blackwell Publishing, 2003), 110.

3. Roderick F. Nash, *Wilderness & the American Mind*, 4th ed. (New Haven: Yale University Press, 2001), 1–2.

4. Opie, *Nature's Nation*, 15.

5. Nash, *Wilderness*, 14–15.

6. William Cronon, "The Trouble with Wilderness, or, Getting back to the Wrong Nature," in *American Environmental History*, 215.

7. According to Roderick Nash, "subjugation of the wilderness was the chief source of pioneer pride." Nash, *Wilderness*, 42.

8. Cronon, "The Trouble with Wilderness," 224.

9. Melanie Perreault, "American Wilderness and First Contact," in *American Wilderness: A New History*, ed. Michael Lewis (Oxford: Oxford University Press, 2007), 23.

10. Raymond W. Stedman, *Shadows of the Indian: Stereotypes in American Culture* (Norman: University of Oklahoma Press, 1982), 6; Richard Drinnon, *Facing West: The Metaphysics of Indian-Hating & Empire Building* (Norman: University of Oklahoma Press, 1997), 136; Karl Jacoby, *Crimes against Nature: Squatters, Poachers, Thieves, and the Hidden History of American Conservation* (Berkeley: University of California Press, 2001), 92.

11. For the genocidal means that the developing American culture tried to deal with Native Americans, see, for example, Drinnon, *Facing West*; Colin G. Calloway, *New Worlds for All: Indians, Europeans, and the Remaking of Early America* (Baltimore: The Johns Hopkins University Press, 1997); Brian W. Dippie, *The Vanishing American: White Attitudes and U.S. Indian Policy* (Lawrence: University Press of Kansas, 1982).

12. Quoted in Ted Steinberg, *Down to Earth: Nature's Role in American History*, 3rd ed. (Oxford: Oxford University Press, 2013), 125–126.

13. Carolyn Merchant, *American Environmental History: An Introduction* (New York: Columbia University Press, 2007), 20.

14. Jim Cullen, *The American Dream: A Short History of an Idea that Shaped a Nation* (Oxford: Oxford University Press, 2003), 23–24.

15. John Winthrop, "A Model of Christian Charity," Collections of the Massachusetts Historical Society, http://history.hanover.edu/texts/winthmod.html, accessed May 15, 2015.

16. Roderick F. Nash, "The Conservation Impulse, Beginnings—1878," in *American Environmentalism: Readings in Conservation History*, ed. Roderick F. Nash, 3rd ed. (New York: McGraw-Hill, Inc., 1990), 9–10.

17. Steinberg, *Down to Earth*, 33–35.

18. Douglas Brinkley, *The Wilderness Warrior: Theodore Roosevelt and the Crusade for America* (New York: Harper Perennial, 2009), 10–11; William T. Hornaday, *Wild Life Conservation in Theory and Practice* (New York: Arno Press, 1972), 12.

19. George P. Marsh, *Man and Nature*, ed. David Lowenthal (Cambridge: The Belknap Press of Harvard University Press, 1965), 80.

20. Merchant, *American Environmental History*, 29, 42–43.

21. Jack Shepherd, *The Forest Killers: The Destruction of the American Wilderness* (New York: Weybright and Talley, 1975), 14–15.

22. Susan Senecah, "Forever Wild or Forever in Battle: Metaphors of Empowerment in the Continuing Controversy over the Adirondacks," in *EarthTalk: Communication Empowerment for Environmental Action*, eds. Star A. Muir and Thomas L. Veenendall (Westport: Praeger, 1996), 98.

23. Merchant, *American Environmental History*, 31.

24. Dan Plazak, *A Hole in the Ground with a Liar at the Top: Fraud and Deceit in the Golden Age of American Mining* (Salt Lake City: The University of Utah Press, 2006), 1.

25. Gordon M. Bakken, *The Mining Law of 1872: Past, Politics, and Prospects* (Albuquerque: University of New Mexico Press, 2008), 55, 96, 100–101.

26. Opie, *Nature's Nation*, 61.

27. Land regulation fell along racial lines with nonwhite groups largely unable to participate. For example, African American slaves could not own land, and, even after their freedom, were physically and economically victimized even if they acquired land. Native Americans, after their military defeat, were for the most part consigned to inadequately sized, infertile lands. See Thomas F. Gossett, *Race: The History of an Idea in America*, New Edition (New York: Oxford University Press, 1997), 255–257; Colin G. Calloway, ed., *Our Hearts Fell to the Ground: Plains Indian Views of How the West Was Lost* (Boston: Bedford Books/St. Martin's Press, 1996), 18.

28. Merchant, *American Environmental History*, 136–137.

29. Steinberg, *Down to Earth*, 134–135; Opie, *Nature's Nation*, 105.

30. William K. Wyant, *Westward in Eden: The Public Lands and the Conservation Movement* (Berkeley: University of California Press, 1982), 18–19.

31. Opie, *Nature's Nation*, 310.

32. Henry N. Smith, *Virgin Land: The American West as Symbol and Myth* (Cambridge: Harvard University Press, 1978), 205.

33. Steinberg, *Down to Earth*, 128–131.

34. Merchant, *American Environmental History*, 137; Frank E. Smith, *The Politics of Conservation* (New York: Pantheon Books, 1966), 53.

35. Wyant, *Westward in Eden*, 61–62.

36. Wyant, *Westward in Eden*, 42.

37. Smith, *The Politics of Conservation*, 52–53.

38. Smith, *The Politics of Conservation*, 54; J. B. Crawford, *The Credit Mobilier of America: Its Origin and History, Its Work of Constructing the Union Pacific Railroad and the Relation of Members of Congress Therewith* (Boston: C. W. Calkins & Co., 1880), 9–16.

39. Wyant, *Westward in Eden*, 37–38.

40. Steinberg, *Down to Earth*, 111–113.

41. Nash, *Wilderness*, 85–86.

42. Ralph W. Emerson, "Nature," (James Munroe & Co., 1836) Accessed at Internet Archive, May 15, 2015, https://archive.org/stream/naturemunroe00emerrich/naturemunroe00emerrich_djvu.txt, May 15.

43. Bradley Dean, "Natural History, Romanticism, and Thoreau," in *American Wilderness: A New History*, ed. Michael Lewis (Oxford: Oxford University Press, 2007), 78–84.

44. Cronon, "The Trouble with Wilderness," 217–219.

45. Merchant, *American Environmental History*, 74.

46. Gregory Clark, S. Michael Halloran, and Allison Woodford, "Thomas Cole's Vision of 'Nature' and the Conquest Theme in American Culture," in *Green Culture: Environmental Rhetoric in Contemporary America*, eds. Carl G. Herndl and Stuart C. Brown (Madison: The University of Wisconsin Press, 1996), 261.

47. Opie, *Nature's Nation*, 204.

48. Steven Stoll, "Farm Against Forest," in *American Wilderness*, 65.

49. Marsh, *Man and Nature*, 42–43.

50. Char Miller, *Gifford Pinchot and the Making of Modern Environmentalism* (Washington: Island Press, 2001), 55–57, 81–86, 134–138.

51. Gifford Pinchot, *The Fight for Conservation* (Seattle: University of Washington Press, 1910), 40–50.

52. See Ray A. Billington, *America's Frontier Heritage* (San Francisco: Holt, Rinehart and Winston, 1966), 12–13; Smith, *Virgin Land*, 250–251; and Ronald H. Carpenter, *The Eloquence of Frederick Jackson Turner* (San Marino: The Huntington Library, 1983), 35–36.

53. Frederick Jackson Turner, *The Significance of the Frontier in American History* (1921; repr., Project Gutenberg, 2007) accessed May 15, 2015, http://www.gutenberg.org/files/22994/22994-h/22994-h.htm#Page_1.

54. Timothy Egan, *The Big Burn: Teddy Roosevelt and the Fire that Saved America* (Boston: Mariner Books, 2009), 33–34.

55. Although Roderick Nash observed that Yellowstone's "initial advocates were not concerned with wilderness; they acted to prevent private acquisition and exploitation of geysers, hot springs, waterfalls, and similar curiosities." The outcome still coincided with the perceived necessity to preserve and/or conserve various facets of the environment; see Nash, *Wilderness*, 108.

56. T. J. Jackson Lears, *No Place of Grace: Antimodernism and the Transformation of American Culture, 1880–1920* (New York: Pantheon Books, 1981), 47–55; Gail Bederman, *Manliness & Civilization: A Cultural History of Gender and Race in the United States, 1880–1917* (Chicago: University of Chicago Press, 1995), 13–14.

57. Jacoby, *Crimes against Nature*, 83, 103, 107.

58. Benjamin Johnson, "Wilderness Parks and Their Discontents," in *American Wilderness*, 114–115.

59. Steinberg, *Down to Earth*, 150.

60. Jacoby, *Crimes against Nature*, 107–110, 119.

61. Merchant, *American Environmental History*, 165.

62. Nash, *Wilderness*, 113.

63. Jacoby, *Crimes against Nature*, 119.

64. Nash, *Wilderness*, 122.

65. Theodore Roosevelt, *An Autobiography* (New York: Charles Scribner's Sons, 1929), 13–19.

66. Roosevelt, *An Autobiography*, 29–31.

67. Douglas Brinkley, *The Wilderness Warrior: Theodore Roosevelt and the Crusade for America* (New York: Harper Perennial, 2009), 30–31, 36.

68. Paul Cutright, *Theodore Roosevelt: The Making of a Conservationist* (Urbana: University of Illinois Press, 1985), 108–109, 127–128.

69. Roosevelt, *An Autobiography*, 93.

70. Brinkley, *The Wilderness Warrior*, 37–38.

71. See Theodore Roosevelt, *Hunting Trips of a Ranchman*, (1885; repr., New York: Bartleby.com, 1999), accessed May 15, 2015, http://www.bartleby.com/52/3.html.

72. Roosevelt, *Hunting Trips of a Ranchman*.

73. Steinberg, *Down to Earth*, 136.

74. Cutright, *Theodore Roosevelt: The Making*, 167–169.

75. Brinkley, *The Wilderness Warrior*, 259–260.

76. Theodore Roosevelt, *The Wilderness Hunter*, in *The Wilderness Hunter; Outdoor Pastimes of an American Hunter*, in The Works of Theodore Roosevelt, National Edition, vol. XV (New York: Charles Scribner's Sons, 1926), xxix, 31, 173.

77. Theodore Roosevelt, "Annual Message, January 2, 1899," in *State Papers as Governor and President 1899–1909*, in The Works of Theodore Roosevelt, National Edition, vol. XV (New York: Charles Scribner's Sons, 1926), 21–22. Hereafter cited as *State Papers*.

78. Brinkley, *The Wilderness Warrior*, 342–345, 352, 356–357; Theodore Roosevelt, "Annual Message, January 3, 1900," *State Papers*, 53–55.

79. Edmund Morris, *The Rise of Theodore Roosevelt* (New York: The Modern Library, 2001), 771, 778–779.

80. Edmund Morris, *Theodore Rex* (New York: Random House, 2001), 22.

81. Quoted in Goodwin, *The Bully Pulpit*, 292; Theodore Roosevelt, *Ranch Life and the Hunting-Trail* (1888; repr., Lincoln: University of Nebraska Press, 1983), 86–97.

82. Roosevelt, *Ranch Life and the Hunting-Trail*, 100.

83. Roosevelt, *Ranch Life and the Hunting-Trail*, 88.

84. Brinkley, *The Wilderness Warrior*, 383.

85. Michael McGerr, *A Fierce Discontent: The Rise and Fall of the Progressive Movement in America, 1870–1920* (Oxford: Oxford University Press, 2003), 17, 32–33, 152–153; Roy Rosenzweig, *Eight Hours for What We Will: Workers & Leisure in an Industrial City, 1870–1920* (Cambridge: Cambridge University Press, 1987), 171–190.

86. David B. Danbom, *"The World of Hope:" Progressives and the Struggle for an Ethical Public Life* (Philadelphia: Temple University Press, 1987), 27–28, 39–79.

87. McGerr, *A Fierce Discontent*, 104–106, 164.

88. For Roosevelt's engagement with the progressive movement, see Leroy G. Dorsey, "Preaching Morality in Modern America: Theodore Roosevelt's Rhetorical Progressivism," in *Rhetoric and Reform in the Progressive Era*, ed. J. Michael Hogan (East Lansing: Michigan State University Press, 2003), 49–83; Sidney M. Milkis, *Theodore Roosevelt, the Progressive Party, and the Transformation of American Democracy* (Lawrence: University Press of Kansas, 2009), 27–74.

89. Theodore Roosevelt, "First Annual Message (1901)," in *State Papers*, 102–108.

90. "The Roosevelt Pets," The National Park Service online video, accessed May 15, 2015, http://www.nps.gov/thrb/historyculture/the-roosevelt-pets.htm.

91. Brinkley, *The Wilderness Warrior*, 492–493.

92. Paul R. Cutright, *Theodore Roosevelt: The Naturalist* (New York: Harper & Brothers: 1956), 179.

93. Morris, *Theodore Rex*, 172–174; Nash, *Wilderness*, 152–153.

94. Brinkley, *The Wilderness Warrior*, 588, 624.

95. For information on Roosevelt's complex racial attitudes toward Native Americans, see Leroy G. Dorsey, *We Are All Americans, Pure and Simple: Theodore Roosevelt and the Myth of Americanism* (Tuscaloosa: The University of Alabama Press, 2007), 69–92.

96. Brinkley, *The Wilderness Warrior*, 581, 595.

97. Roosevelt was not completely innocent as he contributed his share of depictions identifying Native Americans as savages; see Dorsey, *We Are All Americans*, 69–92.

98. Elmo R. Richardson, *The Politics of Conservation: Crusades and Controversies, 1897–1913* (Berkeley: University of California Press, 1962), 19.

99. Cutright, *Theodore Roosevelt: The Naturalist*, 167–168.

100. For the political clash between the aesthetic and the practical surrounding this project, see Christine Oravec, "Conservationism vs. Preservationism: The 'Public Interest' in the Hetch Hetchy Controversy," *Quarterly Journal of Speech* 70 (1984): 444–458.

101. Stephen Fox, *The American Conservation Movement: John Muir and His Legacy* (Madison: The University of Wisconsin Press, 1985), 103–111; Brinkley, *The Wilderness Warrior*, 536–537.

102. Nash, *Wilderness*, 161; Fox, *The American Conservation Movement*, 140–141; Miller, *Gifford Pinchot*, 139; Theodore Roosevelt, "At a Meeting of the Society of American Foresters, Held at the Residence of Mr. Gifford Pinchot, Washington, D. C., March 26, 1903," in *Presidential Addresses and State Papers*, Homeward Bound Edition, volume 1 (New York: The Review of Reviews Company, 1910), 249.

103. Nash, *Wilderness*, 163–180; Brinkley, *The Wilderness Warrior*, 751.

104. Hays, *Conservation and the Gospel of Efficiency*, 67–75.

105. Theodore Roosevelt, "Message Communicated to the Two Houses of Congress, February 13, 1907," in *Presidential Addresses and State Papers*, volume VI, 1160.

106. Hays, *Conservation and the Gospel of Efficiency*, 85–87.

107. Smith, *The Politics of Conservation*, 98–99.

108. Egan, *The Big Burn*, 39–40, 46–49.

109. Theodore Roosevelt, "Remarks at Leland Stanford Jr. University, Palo Alto California, May 12, 1903," in *California Addresses by President Roosevelt* (San Francisco: The California Promotion Committee, 1903), 68–69, 71.

110. Egan, *The Big Burn*, 50.

111. Brinkley, *The Wilderness Warrior*, 678–679. See also William H. Harbaugh, *The Life and Times of Theodore Roosevelt* (New York: Collier Books, 1963), 312–313.

112. Brinkley, *The Wilderness Warrior*, 450–451, 506; 642–643, 754.

113. Theodore Roosevelt, "To the School Children of the United States, April 15, 1907,"

in *Presidential Addresses and State Papers*, volume VI, 1208; Brinkley, *The Wilderness Warrior*, 683–684. For more information about Roosevelt's use of biblical imagery to frame conservation efforts, see Leroy G. Dorsey, "Preaching Conservation: Theodore Roosevelt and the Rhetoric of Civil Religion," in *Green Talk in the White House: The Rhetorical Presidency Encounters Ecology*, ed. Tarla R. Peterson (College Station: Texas A&M University Press, 2004), 37–61.

114. Theodore Roosevelt, "The Campaign Against Privilege, January 31, 1908," in *The Roosevelt Policy: Speeches, Letters and State Papers, related to Corporate Wealth and Closely Allied Topics*, ed. William Griffith, volume 2 (1919; repr., New York: Kraus Reprint Co, 1971), 722, 725

115. Brinkley, *The Wilderness Warrior*, 754–755, 759–760.

CHAPTER THREE

1. Doris Kearns Goodwin, *The Bully Pulpit: Theodore Roosevelt, William Howard Taft, and the Golden Age of Journalism* (New York: Simon & Schuster, 2013), 292–293.

2. Theodore Roosevelt, *An Autobiography* (New York: Charles Scribner's Sons, 1929), 349–350.

3. Roosevelt, *An Autobiography*, 357, 361–363, 386.

4. See, for example, Leroy G. Dorsey, "Preaching Morality in Modern America: Theodore Roosevelt's Rhetorical Progressivism," in *Rhetoric and Reform in the Progressive Era*, ed. J. Michael Hogan (East Lansing: Michigan State University Press, 2003), 49–83; and Joshua D. Hawley, *Theodore Roosevelt: Preacher of Righteousness* (New Haven: Yale University Press, 2008).

5. Roosevelt, *An Autobiography*, 358–359, 361–362.

6. For Roosevelt's rhetorical engagement with Native American issues, see Leroy G. Dorsey, *We Are All Americans, Pure and Simple: Theodore Roosevelt and the Myth of Americanism* (Tuscaloosa: The University of Alabama Press, 2007), 69–92.

7. Roosevelt, *An Autobiography*, 374.

8. Roosevelt, *An Autobiography*, 351, 354, 358.

9. James W. Ceaser, Glen E. Thurow, Jeffrey Tulis, and Joseph M. Bessette, "The Rise of the Rhetorical Presidency," *Presidential Studies Quarterly* 11.2 (1981): 159, 161, 164, 170. Ceaser et al. identified two other modern elements responsible for the rise of the rhetorical presidency: a changing conception of what presidential leadership meant, along with presidential politics becoming a non-stop campaign for reelection. This analysis will connect the presidential leadership element to the discussion of Roosevelt's use of the mass media. However, since Roosevelt announced in his second term—his first full term—that he would not be running for reelection, that non-stop campaign element is not a relevant marker for this analysis.

10. Jeffrey Tulis, *The Rhetorical Presidency* (Princeton: Princeton University Press, 1987), 19, 106, 114, 181.

11. For example, see David Zarefsky, "The Presidency Has Always Been a Place for Rhetorical Leadership," in *The Presidency and Rhetorical Leadership*, ed. Leroy G. Dorsey (2002; repr., College Station: Texas A&M University Press, 2008), 20–41; Stephen E. Lucas, "George Washington and the Rhetoric of Presidential Leadership," in *The Presidency and Rhetorical Leadership*, 42–72; James M. Farrell, "Classical Virtue and Presidential Fame: John Adams, Leadership, and the Franco-American Crisis," in *The Presidency and Rhetorical Leadership*, 73–94; Martin J. Medhurst, ed., *Before the Rhetorical Presidency* (College Station: Texas A&M University Press, 2008); Richard J. Ellis and Alexis Walker, "Policy Speech in the Nineteenth Century Rhetorical Presidency: The

Case of Zachary Taylor's 1849 Tour," *Presidential Studies Quarterly* 37.2 (2007): 248–269; Melvin C. Laracey, *Presidents and the People: The Partisan Story of Going Public* (College Station: Texas A&M University Press, 2002); and Robert P. Saldin, "William McKinley and the Rhetorical Presidency," *Presidential Studies Quarterly* 41.1 (2011): 119–134.

12. Martin J. Medhurst, "Was There a Nineteenth-Century Rhetorical Presidency? A Debate Revisited," in *Before the Rhetorical Presidency*, 2–3.

13. Martin J. Medhurst, "Afterword: The Ways of Rhetoric," in *Beyond the Rhetorical Presidency*, ed. Martin J. Medhurst (College Station: Texas A&M University Press, 1996), 219.

14. Morris, *Theodore Rex*, 131–137; Hawley, *Theodore Roosevelt*, 173–174.

15. William H. Harbaugh, *The Life and Times of Theodore Roosevelt* (New York: Collier Books, 1963), 294.

16. Ralph H. Lutts, *The Nature Fakers: Wildlife, Science & Sentiment* (Charlottesville: The University Press of Virginia, 2001), 102–103.

17. Theodore Roosevelt, "Men Who Misinterpret Nature," in *Through the Brazilian Wilderness and Papers on Natural History*, The Works of Theodore Roosevelt, National Edition, vol. V (New York: Charles Scribner's Sons, 1926), 367, 370, 374.

18. "ROOSEVELT ONLY A GAMEKILLER—LONG," *The New York Times*, May 23, 1907, ProQuest Historical Newspapers, 6.

19. "LONG WRITES ROOSEVELT," *The New York Times*, May 24, 1907, ProQuest Historical Newspapers, 2.

20. Lutts, *The Nature Fakers*, 109–112.

21. Theodore Roosevelt, "Nature-Fakers, September, 1907," in *Through the Brazilian Wilderness and Papers on Natural History*, The Works of Theodore Roosevelt, National Edition, vol. V (New York: Charles Scribner's Sons, 1926), 375, 377–378, 382.

22. Lutts, *The Nature Fakers*, 128–131.

23. Leroy G. Dorsey, "Introduction: The President as a Rhetorical Leader," in *The Presidency and Rhetorical Leadership*, ed. Leroy G. Dorsey (2002; repr., College Station: Texas A&M University Press, 2008), 9–13.

24. Roosevelt, *An Autobiography*, 386.

25. Mary Stuckey, "Establishing the Rhetorical Presidency through Presidential Rhetoric: Theodore Roosevelt and the Brownsville Raid," *Quarterly Journal of Speech* 92.3 (2006): 288.

26. Roosevelt, *An Autobiography*, 404–405.

27. Quoted in Carl E. Hatch, *The Big Stick and The Congressional Gavel: A Study of Theodore Roosevelt's Relations with his Last Congress, 1907–1909* (New York: Pageant Press, Inc., 1967), 13, 15.

28. Roosevelt, *An Autobiography*, 395–396.

29. Medhurst, "Introduction—A Tale of Two Constructs: The Rhetorical Presidency Versus Presidential Rhetoric," in *Beyond the Rhetorical Presidency*, xii–xiv.

30. Ceaser et al., "The Rise of the Rhetorical Presidency," 164.

31. George Juergens, *News From the White House* (Chicago: The University of Chicago Press, 1981), 14, 16.

32. Douglas Brinkley, *The Wilderness Warrior: Theodore Roosevelt and the Crusade for America* (New York: Harper Perennial, 2009), 682.

33. David S. Barry, *Forty Years in Washington* (1924; New York: Beekman Publishers Inc., 1974), 270–271. For an example of Roosevelt's orchestration of media stories regarding his agenda, see Leroy G. Dorsey, "Sailing into the 'Wondrous Now': The Myth of the American Navy's World Cruise," *Quarterly Journal of Speech* 83 (1997): 447–465.

34. Brinkley, *The Wilderness Warrior*, 683.

35. Juergens, *News From the White House*, 67; Samuel Kernell, *Going Public: New Strategies of Presidential Leadership*, 3rd edition (Washington: Congressional Quarterly Inc., 1997), 75.

36. Karlyn K. Campbell and Kathleen H. Jamieson, *Presidents Creating the Presidency: Deeds Done in Words* (Chicago: The University of Chicago Press, 2008), 137–138.

37. Campbell and Jamieson, *Presidents Creating the Presidency*, 137, 139–150.

38. For example, see Leroy G. Dorsey, *We Are All Americans, Pure and Simple: Theodore Roosevelt and the Myth of Americanism* (Tuscaloosa: The University of Alabama Press, 2007); Dorsey, "Sailing into the 'Wondrous Now,' 447–465; Leroy G. Dorsey, "Managing Women's Equality: Theodore Roosevelt, the Frontier Myth, and the Modern Woman," *Rhetoric & Public Affairs* 16.3 (2013): 423–456.

39. For examinations of Roosevelt's history as a rhetorical force, see Leroy G. Dorsey and Rachel M. Harlow, "'We Want Americans Pure and Simple': Theodore Roosevelt and the Myth of Americanism," *Rhetoric & Public Affairs* 6.1 (2003): 55–78.

40. Theodore Roosevelt, *The Wining of the West: An Account of the Exploration and Settlement of Our Country from the Alleghanies to the Pacific*, The Works of Theodore Roosevelt, National Edition, vol. VIII (New York: Charles Scribner's Sons, 1926), 28.

41. Roosevelt, *The Wining of the West*, 100, 116.

42. Roosevelt, *The Wining of the West*, 72; Theodore Roosevelt, *The Wining of the West: An Account of the Exploration and Settlement of Our Country from the Alleghanies to the Pacific*, The Works of Theodore Roosevelt, National Edition, vol. IX (New York: Charles Scribner's Sons, 1926), 56–57.

43. Roosevelt, *The Wining of the West*, 143.

44. For more information on Roosevelt's altering of the Frontier Myth to popularize the farmer as a conservationist hero, see Leroy G. Dorsey, "The Frontier Myth in Presidential Rhetoric: Theodore Roosevelt's Campaign for Conservation," *Western Journal of Communication* 59 (1995), 1–19. The literature on the Frontier Myth is quite extensive, but one key example is Richard Slotkin's massive three-volume work tracing that myth's influence in American culture over several centuries—*Regeneration Through Violence: The Mythology of the American Frontier, 1600–1860* (Norman: University of Oklahoma Press, 1973); *The Fatal Environment: The Myth of the Frontier in the Age of Industrialization, 1800–1890* (Norman: University of Oklahoma Press, 1985/1998); and *Gunfighter Nation: The Myth of the Frontier in Twentieth-Century America* (New York: Atheneum, 1992).

45. Bruce Lincoln, *Discourse and the Construction of Society: Comparative Studies of Myth, Ritual, and Classification* (New York: Oxford University Press, 1989), 24–25; Slotkin, *Regeneration Through Violence*, 8–9.

CHAPTER FOUR

1. Gifford Pinchot, *Breaking New Ground* (New York: Harcourt, Brace and Company, 1947), 150–151.

2. Theodore Roosevelt, "At a Meeting of the Society of American Foresters," in *Presidential Addresses and State Papers*, Homeward Bound Edition, Volume I, (New York: The Review of Reviews Company, MCMX), 249–257.

3. Pinchot, *Breaking New Ground*, 151. See "CARE OF THE FORESTS," *Evening Star*, March 27, 1903, 17, in Chronicling America: Historic American Newspapers. Lib. of Congress, http://chroniclingamerica.loc.gov/lccn/sn83045462/1903–03–27/ed-1/seq-17/; "The President at Meeting of American Foresters," *The Sun*, March 27, 1903, 2; in Chronicling America: Historic American Newspapers. Lib. of Congress, http://chroniclingamerica.loc.gov/lccn/sn83030272/1903–03–27/ed-1/seq-2/; "PRESIDENT'S THEME WAS CARE OF FORESTS," *The Washington Times*, March 27, 1903, 2, in Chronicling America: Historic American

Newspapers. Lib. of Congress, http://chroniclingamerica.loc.gov/lccn/sn84026749/1903–03–27/ed-1/seq-2/.

4. Pinchot, *Breaking New Ground*, 254; Char Miller, *Gifford Pinchot and the Making of Modern Environmentalism* (Washington: Island Press, 2001), 196.

5. Theodore Roosevelt, "Forestry and Business," in *American Problems*, in The Works of Theodore Roosevelt, National Edition, vol. XVI (New York: Charles Scribner's Sons, 1926), 101–102, 106.

6. See, for example, "MANY NOTABLES HEAR PRESIDENT," *Los Angeles Herald*, January 6, 1905, 2, in Chronicling America: Historic American Newspapers. Lib. of Congress, http://chroniclingamerica.loc.gov/lccn/sn85042462/1905–01–06/ed-1/seq-2/; "MUST PROTECT THE WOODLANDS," *The Salt Lake Tribune*, January 4, 1905, 2, in Chronicling America: Historic American Newspapers. Lib. of Congress, http://chroniclingamerica.loc.gov/lccn/sn83045396/1905–01–04/ed-1/seq-2/; "RIVER AND HARBOR BILL," *The Norfolk Weekly News Journal*, January 6, 1905, 1, in Chronicling America: Historic American Newspapers. Lib. of Congress, http://chroniclingamerica.loc.gov/lccn/sn95070058/1905–01–06/ed-1/seq-1/.

7. Douglas Brinkley, *The Wilderness Warrior: Theodore Roosevelt and the Crusade for America* (New York: Harper Perennial, 2009), 691–692.

8. Theodore Roosevelt, "Before the National Editorial Association at Jamestown, VA., June 10, 1907," in *Presidential Addresses and State Papers*, Homeward Bound Edition, Volume VI, (New York: The Review of Reviews Company, MCMX), 1308, 1311.

9. See, for example, "PRESIDENT READY FOR GEORGIA DAY," *The Times Dispatch*, June 10, 1907, 1, in Chronicling America: Historic American Newspapers. Lib. of Congress, http://chroniclingamerica.loc.gov/lccn/sn85038615/1907–06–10/ed-1/seq-1/; "ROOSEVELT IDEAL NEWSPAPER MAN," *The Spokane Press*, June 10, 1907, 1, in Chronicling America: Historic American Newspapers. Lib. of Congress, http://chroniclingamerica.loc.gov/lccn/sn88085947/1907–06–10/ed-1/seq-1/; "GALA FETE DAY AT JAMESTOWN FOR OLD GEORGIA," *The Evening Star*, June 10, 1907, 1, in Chronicling America: Historic American Newspapers. Lib. of Congress, http://chroniclingamerica.loc.gov/lccn/sn83045462/1907–06–10/ed-1/seq-1/.

10. Roosevelt, "Before the National Editorial Association," 1310.

11. Samuel P. Hays, *Conservation and the Gospel of Efficiency: The Progressive Conservation Movement, 1890–1920* (Pittsburgh: University of Pittsburgh Press, 1999), 138–139.

12. Jeffrey K. Tulis, *The Rhetorical Presidency* (Princeton: Princeton University Press, 1987), 181.

13. Edmund Morris, *Theodore Rex* (New York: Random House, 2001), 496; Brinkley, *The Wilderness Warrior*, 693; Stephen Ponder, "Federal News Management in the Progressive Era: Gifford Pinchot and the Conservation Crusade," *Journalism History* 13.2 (1986): 45.

14. "ROOSEVELT URGES DEEP WATERWAYS," *The Washington Herald*, October 3, 1907, 1, in Chronicling America: Historic American Newspapers. Lib. of Congress, http://chroniclingamerica.loc.gov/lccn/sn83045433/1907–10–03/ed-1/seq-1/; "PRESIDENT IN RAIN," *The Omaha Daily Bee*, October 3, 1907, 1, in Chronicling America: Historic American Newspapers. Lib. of Congress, http://chroniclingamerica.loc.gov/lccn/sn99021999/1907–10–03/ed-1/seq-1/.

15. Theodore Roosevelt, "At St. Louis, MO., October 2, 1907," in *Presidential Addresses and State Papers*, Homeward Bound Edition, Volume VI, (New York: The Review of Reviews Company, MCMX), 1390–1391; Theodore Roosevelt, "At Cairo, Ill., October 3, 1907," in *Presidential Addresses and State Papers*, Volume VI, 1417–1419.

16. Morris, *Theodore Rex*, 496.

17. Theodore Roosevelt, "To the Deep Waterway Convention at Memphis, Tenn., October 4, 1907," in *Presidential Addresses and State Papers*, Homeward Bound Edition, Volume VI, (New York: The Review of Reviews Company, MCMX), 1425, 1432–1433.

18. Brinkley, *The Wilderness Warrior*, 692.

19. "Consternation in Louisiana," *Albuquerque Citizen*, October 4, 1907, 1, in Chronicling America: Historic American Newspapers. Lib. of Congress. http://chroniclingamerica.loc.gov/lccn/sn84020616/1907–10–04/ed-1/seq-1/; "Panic in the Cane Brake," *The Evening Star*, October 4, 1907, 1, in Chronicling America: Historic American Newspapers. Lib. of Congress, http://chroniclingamerica.loc.gov/lccn/sn83045462/1907–10–04/ed-1/seq-1/.

20. Morris, *Theodore Rex*, 497.

21. "Life on the Mississippi," *The Evening Star*, October 2, 1907, 1, in Chronicling America: Historic American Newspapers. Lib. of Congress, http://chroniclingamerica.loc.gov/lccn/sn83045462/1907–10–02/ed-1/seq-1/; "Improve Rivers, Build Navy, and Fight Big Corporations, Says Roosevelt in Memphis," *The Washington Times*, October 5, 1907, 6, in Chronicling America: Historic American Newspapers. Lib. of Congress, http://chroniclingamerica.loc.gov/lccn/sn84026749/1907–10–05/ed-1/seq-6/; "ROOSEVELT MAKES BIG SPEECH AT DEEP WATER WAYS CONVENTION—IS SARCASTIC AT WALL STREET," *Bismarck Daily Tribune*, October 5, 1907, 1, in Chronicling America: Historic American Newspapers. Lib. of Congress, http://chroniclingamerica.loc.gov/lccn/sn85042242/1907–10–05/ed-1/seq-1/.

22. Ponder, "Federal News Management in the Progressive Era," 44.

23. "ROOSEVELT CALLS FOR MEETING OF GOVERNORS," *The San Francisco Call*, November 18, 1907, 4, in Chronicling America: Historic American Newspapers. Lib. of Congress. http://chroniclingamerica.loc.gov/lccn/sn85066387/1907–11–18/ed-1/seq-4/.

24. According to Campbell and Jamieson, the appearance of the congressional and executive branches during the State of the Union "encourages a cooperative relationship between them"—see *Presidents Creating the Presidency*, 163.

25. See W. J. McGee, *Proceeding of a Conference of Governors, in the White House, Washington, D. C., May 13–15, 1908* (New York: Arno Press, 1972), xix–xxxi; Pinchot, *Breaking New Ground*, 345–346.

26. "ALL ROADS TO WHITE HOUSE," *The Omaha Daily Bee*, May 5, 1908, 2, in Chronicling America: Historic American Newspapers. Lib. of Congress, http://chroniclingamerica.loc.gov/lccn/sn99021999/1908–05–05/ed-1/seq-2/; "BIG MEN GATHER FOR CONFERENCE," *The Evening Statesman*, May 12, 1908, in Chronicling America: Historic American Newspapers. Lib. of Congress, http://chroniclingamerica.loc.gov/lccn/sn88085421/1908–05–12/ed-1/seq-1/.

27. "CONFERENCE OF GOVERNORS AT WASHINGTON MAY 13," *The Bisbee Daily Review*, May 2, 1908, 8, in Chronicling America: Historic American Newspapers. Lib. of Congress, http://chroniclingamerica.loc.gov/lccn/sn84024827/1908–05–02/ed-1/seq-8/; "GATHERING OF THE GOVERNORS," *Deseret Evening News*, May 8, 1908, 1, in Chronicling America: Historic American Newspapers. Lib. of Congress, http://chroniclingamerica.loc.gov/lccn/sn83045555/1908–05–08/ed-1/seq-1/; "GOVERNORS IN CONFERENCE," *The National Tribune*, April 23, 1908, in Chronicling America: Historic American Newspapers. Lib. of Congress, http://chroniclingamerica.loc.gov/lccn/sn82016187/1908–04–23/ed-1/seq-4/; "REMARKABLE CONFERENCE THIS WEEK ON THE HUSBANDING OF AMERICA'S NATURAL RESOURCES," *New-York Tribune*, May 10, 1908, in Chronicling America: Historic American Newspapers. Lib. of Congress, http://chroniclingamerica.loc.gov/lccn/sn83030214/1908–05–10/ed-1/seq-17/; "CONFERENCE TO BE A LOVE FEAST," *Albuquerque Citizen*, May 6, 1908, 6, in

Chronicling America: Historic American Newspapers. Lib. of Congress, http://chroniclingamerica.loc.gov/lccn/sn84020616/1908–05–06/ed-1/seq-6/.

28. "CONFERENCE OF GOVERNORS THIS WEEK," *Albuquerque Citizen*, May 11, 1908, 3, in Chronicling America: Historic American Newspapers. Lib. of Congress, http://chroniclingamerica.loc.gov/lccn/sn84020616/1908–05–11/ed-1/seq-3/. The steady drumbeat of information from the White House itself became a topic of media stories; see Ponder, "Federal News Management," 46.

29. "THE NATION'S RESOURCES," *The Arizona Republican*, May 14, 1908, 1, in Chronicling America: Historic American Newspapers. Lib. of Congress, http://chroniclingamerica.loc.gov/lccn/sn84020558/1908–05–14/ed-1/seq-10/.

30. See, for example, "WASTE OF SOIL AND DEPLETION OF FORESTS," *Daily Press*, May 15, 1908, 1, in Chronicling America: Historic American Newspapers. Lib. of Congress, http://chroniclingamerica.loc.gov/lccn/sn83045830/1908–05–15/ed-1/seq-1/; Pinchot, *Breaking New Ground*, 347.

31. "GOVERNORS MEET AT WHITE HOUSE NEXT WEDNESDAY," *The Washington Times*, May 10, 1908, in Chronicling America: Historic American Newspapers. Lib. of Congress, http://chroniclingamerica.loc.gov/lccn/sn84026749/1908–05–10/ed-1/seq-9/.

32. "PRESIDENT CONFERS WITH GOVERNORS," *New-York Tribune*, May 14, 1908, in Chronicling America: Historic American Newspapers. Lib. of Congress, http://chroniclingamerica.loc.gov/lccn/sn83030214/1908–05–14/ed-1/seq-1/.

33. "CONFERENCE OF GOVERNORS THIS WEEK," *Albuquerque Citizen*, May 11, 1908, 3, in Chronicling America: Historic American Newspapers. Lib. of Congress, http://chroniclingamerica.loc.gov/lccn/sn84020616/1908–05–11/ed-1/seq-3/.

34. "HISTORY MADE," *The Washington Herald*, May 14, 1908, 1, Chronicling America: Historic American Newspapers. Lib. of Congress, http://chroniclingamerica.loc.gov/lccn/sn83045433/1908–05–14/ed-1/seq-1/.

35. "CONFERENCE IS UNPRECEDENTED," *Los Angeles Herald*, May 14, 1908, 1, in Chronicling America: Historic American Newspapers. Lib. of Congress, http://chroniclingamerica.loc.gov/lccn/sn85042462/1908–05–14/ed-1/seq-1/; "CONFERENCE OF GOVERNORS THIS WEEK," *Albuquerque Citizen*, May 11, 1908, 3, in Chronicling America: Historic American Newspapers. Lib. of Congress, http://chroniclingamerica.loc.gov/lccn/sn84020616/1908–05–11/ed-1/seq-3/.

36. McGee, *Proceedings of a Conference of Governors*, 408.

37. Samuel P. Hays, *Conservation and the Gospel of Efficiency: The Progressive Conservation Movement, 1890–1920* (Pittsburgh: University of Pittsburgh Press, 1999), 192–193.

38. "Letter from John Muir et al. to [Theodore Roosevelt], 1908, May 2," in the Holt-Atherton Special Collections, http://digitalcollections.pacific.edu/cdm/ref/collection/muirletters/id/5968.

39. "GREAT HISTORY-MAKING CONFERENCE NOW OPENED," *The Salt Lake Tribune*, May 14, 1908, in Chronicling America: Historic American Newspapers. Lib. of Congress, http://chroniclingamerica.loc.gov/lccn/sn83045396/1908–05–14/ed-1/seq-11/.

40. McGee, *Proceedings of a Conference of Governors*, 1.

41. Theodore Roosevelt, "Opening Address by the President," in McGee, *Proceeding of a Conference of Governors*, 3. All further references from this speech will come from this source.

42. Roosevelt, *An Autobiography*, 357.

43. Richard Slotkin, *Regeneration Through Violence: The Mythology of the American Frontier, 1600–1860* (Norman: University of Oklahoma Press, 1973), 8–9.

44. Karlyn K. Campbell and Kathleen H. Jamieson, *Presidents Creating the Presidency: Deeds Done in Words* (Chicago: The University of Chicago Press, 2008), 139–151.

45. Mircea Eliade, *The Sacred & the Profane: The Nature of Religion*, translated by Willard R. Trask, (San Diego: Harcourt Brace & Company, 1987), 68–69.

46. The Official King James Bible Online, "Jonah," chapter 3, http://www.kingjamesbibleonline.org/Jonah-Chapter-3/; The Official King James Bible Online, "Matthew," chapter 11, http://www.kingjamesbibleonline.org/Matthew-Chapter-11.

47. Paul R. Cutright, *Theodore Roosevelt: The Making of a Conservationist* (Urbana: University of Illinois Press, 1985), 211.

48. Aristotle, *The "Art" of Rhetoric*, translated by John H. Freese, Loeb Classic Library, Volume 22 (Cambridge: Harvard University Press, 1982), 201.

49. Ch. Perelman and L. Olbrechts-Tyteca, *The New Rhetoric: A Treatise on Argumentation*, trans. by John Wilkinson and Purcell Weaver, (Notre Dame: University of Notre Dame Press, 1969), 116–117, 144–145.

50. Richard Slotkin, *The Fatal Environment: The Myth of the Frontier in the Age of Industrialization, 1800–1890* (Norman: University of Oklahoma Press, 1994), 15.

51. Slotkin, *Regeneration Through Violence*, 9.

52. Henry N. Smith, *Virgin Land: The American West as Symbol and Myth* (Cambridge: Harvard University Press, 1978), 134.

53. Morris, *Theodore Rex*, 518.

54. Kathleen H. Jamieson, *Eloquence in an Electronic Age: The Transformation of Political Speechmaking* (New York: Oxford University Press, 121.

55. Campbell and Jamieson, *Presidents Creating the Presidency*, 157–158.

56. Janice H. Rushing, "The Rhetoric of the American Western Myth," *Communication Monographs* 50 (1983): 16.

57. Hudson County Water Company, Plff. In Err., v. Robert H. McCarter, Attorney General of the State of New Jersey, 209 U.S. 349 (28 S.Ct. 529, 52 L.Ed. 828), March 18–19/April 6, 1908, http://www.law.cornell.edu/supremecourt/text/209/349.

58. McGee, *Proceeding of a Conference of Governors*, 13.

59. Brinkley, *The Wilderness Warrior*, 577–578.

60. McGee, *Proceeding of a Conference of Governors*, 14, 20, 24.

61. Ibid., 36, 39, 48, 59–60, 62.

62. See Morris, *Theodore Rex*, 60–61; Leroy G. Dorsey, "Theodore Roosevelt and Corporate America, 1901–1909: A Reexamination," *Presidential Studies Quarterly* 25.4 (1995): 732–733.

63. McGee, *Proceeding of a Conference of Governors*, 69, 74.

64. Ibid., 85–86, 116, 125–126.

65. Ibid., 153, 156.

66. Ibid., 172–173.

67. Ibid., 180–182.

68. Ibid., 192–194.

69. Ibid., 195–201.

70. Ibid., 202–206.

71. Ibid., 213–214, 221, 231, 234–235.

72. "PRESIDENT CONFERS WITH GOVERNORS," *New-York Tribune*, May 14, 1908, 1, Chronicling America: Historic American Newspapers. Lib. of Congress, http://chroniclingamerica.loc.gov/lccn/sn83030214/1908–05–14/ed-1/seq-1/.

73. "PRESIDENT CHEERED BY THE GOVERNORS," *The Washington Times*, May 15, 1908, 1, Chronicling America: Historic American Newspapers. Lib. of Congress, http://chroniclingamerica.loc.gov/lccn/sn84026749/1908–05–15/ed-1/seq-1.

74. "GOVERNORS TAKE TANGIBLE ACTION," *The Washington Herald*, May 15, 1908, 1, Chronicling America: Historic American Newspapers. Lib. of Congress, http://chroniclingamerica.loc.gov/lccn/sn83045433/1908–05–15/ed-1/seq-1/.

75. See "'DECLARATION' IS GOVERNORS' WAY OF SETTLEMENT," *Los Angeles Herald*, May 16, 1908, 1, Chronicling America: Historic American Newspapers. Lib. of Congress, http://chroniclingamerica.loc.gov/lccn/sn85042462/1908–05–16/ed-1/seq-1/; "RIGHTS OF STATES THE GREAT QUESTION," *Daily Press*, May 16, 1908, 1, Chronicling America: Historic American Newspapers. Lib. of Congress, http://chroniclingamerica.loc.gov/lccn/sn83045830/1908–05–16/ed-1/seq-1/; "GOVERNORS PRAISE THE PRESIDENT," *The Salt Lake Herald*, May 16, 1908, 1, Chronicling America: Historic American Newspapers. Lib. of Congress, http://chroniclingamerica.loc.gov/lccn/sn85058130/1908–05–16/ed-1/seq-1/.

CHAPTER FIVE

1. Samuel P. Hays, *Conservation and the Gospel of Efficiency: The Progressive Conservation Movement, 1890–1920* (Pittsburgh: University of Pittsburgh Press, 1999), 138, 140.
2. Ibid., 148–149, 168–169.
3. Patricia O'Toole, *When Trumpets Call: Theodore Roosevelt After the White House* (New York: Simon & Schuster, 2005), 82.
4. Mary Stuckey, "Establishing the Rhetorical Presidency through Presidential Rhetoric: Theodore Roosevelt and the Brownsville Raid," *Quarterly Journal of Speech* 92.3 (2006): 305.
5. Char Miller, *Gifford Pinchot and the Making of Modern Environmentalism* (Washington: Island Press, 2001), 253–258, 269–293.
6. "CONFERENCE OF THE GOVERNORS COMES TO END," *Bisbee Daily Review*, May 16, 1908, 1, Chronicling America: Historic American Newspapers. Lib. of Congress, http://chroniclingamerica.loc.gov/lccn/sn84024827/1908–05–16/ed-1/seq-1/.
7. Cutright, *Theodore Roosevelt: The Naturalist*, 182.
8. "THE GOVERNORS AT WASHINGTON," *The Nation*, volume 86, no. 2238, May 21, 1908: 460.
9. Associated Press, "Cliven Bundy: God Told Me to Fight 'Civil War' Against Feds," *The Huffington Post*, August 3, 2014, http://www.huffingtonpost.com/2014/08/03/cliven-bundy-iap-god-civil-war-_n_5646121.html.
10. Jean Williams, "Climate Change: Too Much Rain Caused Deadly Mudslide on Unstable Ground," *Examiner.com*, March 25, 2014, http://www.examiner.com/article/climate-change-too-much-rain-caused-deadly-mudslide-on-unstable-ground; Chelsea J. Carter, "Catastropic Washington Landslide: Plenty of Blame to Go Around?," *CNN*, April 2, 2014, http://www.cnn.com/2014/04/02/us/washington-landslide-logging-development.
11. Jonathan Kaiman, "China's Toxic Air Pollution Resembles Nuclear Winter, Say Scientists," *The Guardian*, February 25, 2014, http://www.theguardian.com/world/2014/feb/25/china-toxic-air-pollution-nuclear-winter-scientists.
12. David Horsey, "African Elephant Slaughter Nears Tipping Point Toward Extinction," *Los Angeles Times*, August 22, 2014, http://www.latimes.com/opinion/topoftheticket/la-na-tt-african-elephant-slaughter-20140821-story.html.
13. Doug Mataconis, "Rand Paul and Others on the Right Denounce Cliven Bundy," *Outside the Beltway*, April 24, 2014, http://www.outsidethebeltway.com/rand-paul-and-others-on-the-right-denounce-cliven-bundy.
14. Tom Rawle, "Cheerleader Causes Outrage AGAIN Trying to Defend Snaps of Hunted Big-Game Animals," *Daily Star*, July 3, 2014, http://www.dailystar.co.uk/news/latest-news/387042/Cheerleader-defends-killing-and-posing-with-rare-dead-animals.
15. John Abraham and Dana Nuccitelli, "President Obama Gets Serious on Climate Change," *The Guardian*, June 3, 2014, http://www.theguardian.com/environment/climate-consensus-97-per-cent/2014/jun/03/president-obama-gets-serious-on-climate-change.

16. Suzanne Goldenberg, "Barack Obama to Create World's Large Ocean Reserve in the Pacific," *The Guardian*, September 25, 2014, http://www.theguardian.com/environment/2014/sep/25/barack-obama-worlds-largest-ocean-reserve-pacific.

17. William H. Harbaugh, *The Life and Times of Theodore Roosevelt* (New York: Collier Books, 1963), 319.

Select Bibliography

Aristotle. *The "Art" of Rhetoric*. Translated by John H. Freese. Loeb Classic Library, Volume 22. Cambridge: Harvard University Press, 1982.

Bakken, Gordon M. *The Mining Law of 1872: Past, Politics, and Prospects*. Albuquerque: University of New Mexico Press, 2008.

Barry, David. *Forty Years in Washington*. New York: Beekman Publishers Inc., 1974.

Barthes, Roland. *Mythologies*. Translated by Annette Lavers. New York: The Noonday Press, 1972.

Bates, J. Leonard. "Fulfilling American Democracy: The Conservation Movement, 1907 to 1921." *The Mississippi Valley Historical Review* 44.1 (1957): 29–57.

Bederman, Gail. *Manliness & Civilization: A Cultural History of Gender and Race in the United States, 1880–1917*. Chicago: University of Chicago Press, 1995.

Billington, Ray A. *America's Frontier Heritage*. San Francisco: Holt, Rinehart and Winston, 1966.

Brands, H. W. *T.R.: The Last Romantic*. New York: Basic Books, 1997.

Brinkley, Douglas. *The Wilderness Warrior: Theodore Roosevelt and the Crusade for America*. New York: Harper Perennial, 2009.

Burke, Kenneth. *A Rhetoric of Motives*. New York: Prentice-Hall, Inc., 1952.

———. "Revolutionary Symbolism in America." In *The Legacy of Kenneth Burke*, edited by Herbert W. Simons and Trevor Melia, 267–273. Madison: University of Wisconsin Press, 1989.

Brummett, Barry. *Reading Rhetorical Theory*. Fort Worth: Harcourt College Publishers, 2000.

Buehler, Daniel O. "Permanence and Change in Theodore Roosevelt's Conservation Jeremiad." *Western Journal of Communication* 62.4 (1998): 439–458.

Calloway, Colin G. *New Worlds for All: Indians, Europeans, and the Remaking of Early America*. Baltimore: The Johns Hopkins University Press, 1997.

———, ed. *Our Hearts Fell to the Ground: Plains Indian Views of How the West Was Lost*. Boston: Bedford Books/St. Martin's Press, 1996.

Campbell, Karlyn K, and Kathleen H. Jamieson. *Presidents Creating the Presidency: Deeds Done in Words*. Chicago: The University of Chicago Press, 2008.

Carpenter, Ronald H. *The Eloquence of Frederick Jackson Turner*. San Marino: The Huntington Library, 1983.

Ceaser, James W., Glen E. Thurow, Jeffrey Tulis, and Joseph M. Bessette. "The Rise of the Rhetorical Presidency." *Presidential Studies Quarterly* 11.2 (1981): 158–171.

Chidester, Phillip J. "'The Toy Store of Life': Myth, Sport and the Mediated Reconstruction of the American Hero in the Shadow of the September 11th Terrorist Attacks." *Southern Communication Journal* 74.4 (2009): 352–372.

Clark, Gregory, S., Michael Halloran, and Allison Woodford. "Thomas Cole's Vision of 'Nature' and the Conquest Theme in American Culture." In *Green Culture: Environmental Rhetoric in Contemporary America*, edited by Carl G. Herndl and Stuart C. Brown, 261–280. Madison: The University of Wisconsin Press, 1996.

Crawford, J. B. *The Credit Mobilier of America: Its Origin and History, Its Work of Constructing the Union Pacific Railroad and the Relation of Members of Congress Therewith*. Boston: C. W. Calkins & Co., 1880.

Cronon, William. "The Trouble with Wilderness, or, Getting back to the Wrong Nature." In *American Environmental History*, edited by Louis S. Warren, 213–236. Malden: Blackwell Publishing, 2003.

Cullen, Jim. *The American Dream: A Short History of an Idea that Shaped a Nation*. Oxford: Oxford University Press, 2003.

Cutright, Paul R. *Theodore Roosevelt: The Making of a Conservationist*. Urbana: University of Illinois Press, 1985.

———. *Theodore Roosevelt: The Naturalist*. New York: Harper & Brothers, 1956.

Danbom, David B. *"The World of Hope:" Progressives and the Struggle for an Ethical Public Life*. Philadelphia: Temple University Press, 1987.

Dean, Bradley. "Natural History, Romanticism, and Thoreau." In *American Wilderness: A New History*, edited by Michael Lewis, 78–84. Oxford: Oxford University Press, 2007.

Dickinson, Greg, Brian L. Ott, and Eric Aoki. "Memory and Myth at the Buffalo Bill Museum." *Western Journal of Communication* 69.2 (2005): 85–108.

Dippie, Brian W. *Custer's Last Stand: The Anatomy of an American Myth*. Lincoln: University of Nebraska Press, 1976.

———. *The Vanishing American: White Attitudes and U.S. Indian Policy*. Lawrence: University Press of Kansas, 1982.

Dorsey, Leroy G. "Introduction: The President as a Rhetorical Leader." In *The Presidency and Rhetorical Leadership*, edited by Leroy G. Dorsey, 3–19. College Station: Texas A&M University Press, 2002.

———. "Managing Women's Equality: Theodore Roosevelt, the Frontier Myth, and the Modern Woman," *Rhetoric & Public Affairs* 16.3 (2013): 423–456.

———. "Preaching Conservation: Theodore Roosevelt and the Rhetoric of Civil Religion." In *Green Talk in the White House*, edited by Tarla R. Peterson, 37–61. College Station: Texas A&M University Press, 2004.

———. "Preaching Morality in Modern America: Theodore Roosevelt's Rhetorical Progressivism." In *Rhetoric and Reform in the Progressive Era*, edited by J. Michael Hogan, 49–83. East Lansing: Michigan State University Press, 2003.

———. "Sailing into the 'Wondrous Now': The Myth of the American Navy's World Cruise." *Quarterly Journal of Speech* 83 (1997): 447–465.

———. "The Frontier Myth in Presidential Rhetoric: Theodore Roosevelt's Campaign for Conservation." *Western Journal of Communication* 59 (1995): 1–19.

———. "Theodore Roosevelt and Corporate America, 1901–1909: A Reexamination." *Presidential Studies Quarterly* 25.4 (1995): 725–739.

———. "Theodore Roosevelt and the Progressive Impulses of Conservation." In *Green Voices: Defending Nature and the Environment in American Civic Discourse*, edited by Richard D. Besel and Bernard K. Duffy, forthcoming. Albany: State University of New York Press, 2016.

———, ed. *The Presidency and Rhetorical Leadership*. College Station: Texas A&M University Press, 2002.

———. *We Are All Americans, Pure and Simple: Theodore Roosevelt and the Myth of Americanism*. Tuscaloosa: The University of Alabama Press, 2007.

———. "'We Want Americans Pure and Simple': Theodore Roosevelt and the Myth of Americanism." *Rhetoric & Public Affairs* 6.1 (2003): 55–78.

Drinnon, Richard. *Facing West: The Metaphysics of Indian-Hating & Empire Building*. Norman: University of Oklahoma Press, 1997.

Edwards III, George C. *On Deaf Ears: The Limits of the Bully Pulpit.* New Haven: Yale University Press, 2003.

Egan, Timothy. *The Big Burn: Teddy Roosevelt and the Fire That Saved America.* Boston: Mariner Books, 2009.

Eliade, Mircea. *The Sacred & the Profane: The Nature of Religion.* Translated by Willard R. Trask. San Diego: Harcourt Brace & Company, 1987.

Ellis Richard J., and Alexis Walker. "Policy Speech in the Nineteenth Century Rhetorical Presidency: The Case of Zachary Taylor's 1849 Tour." *Presidential Studies Quarterly* 37.2 (2007): 248–269.

Farrell, James M. "Classical Virtue and Presidential Fame: John Adams, Leadership, and the Franco-American Crisis." In *The Presidency and Rhetorical Leadership,* edited by Leroy G. Dorsey, 73–94. College Station: Texas A&M University Press, 2002.

Foss, Sonja K., Karen A. Foss, and Robert Trapp. *Contemporary Perspectives on Rhetoric,* 30th Anniversary Ed. Long Grove: Waveland Press, 2014.

Fox, Stephen. *The American Conservation Movement: John Muir and His Legacy.* Madison: The University of Wisconsin Press, 1985.

Goodwin, Doris Kearns. *The Bully Pulpit: Theodore Roosevelt, William Howard Taft, and the Golden Age of Journalism.* New York: Simon & Schuster, 2013.

Gossett, Thomas F. *Race: The History of an Idea in America,* New Edition. New York: Oxford University Press, 1997.

Gregg II, Gary L. *The Presidential Republic: Executive Representation and Deliberative Democracy.* Lanham: Rowman & Littlefield Publishers, Inc., 1997.

Harbaugh, William H. *The Life and Times of Theodore Roosevelt.* New York: Collier Books, 1963.

Hatch, Carl E. *The Big Stick and The Congressional Gavel: A Study of Theodore Roosevelt's Relations with his Last Congress, 1907–1909.* New York: Pageant Press, Inc., 1967.

Hawley, Joshua D. *Theodore Roosevelt: Preacher of Righteousness.* New Haven: Yale University Press, 2008.

Hays, Samuel P. *Conservation and the Gospel of Efficiency: The Progressive Conservation Movement, 1890–1920.* Pittsburgh: University of Pittsburgh Press, 1999.

Hornaday, William T. *Wild Life Conservation in Theory and Practice.* New York: Arno Press, 1972.

Hughes, Richard T. *Myths America Lives By.* Urbana: University of Illinois Press, 2003.

Jacoby, Karl. *Crimes against Nature: Squatters, Poachers, Thieves, and the Hidden History of American Conservation.* Berkeley: University of California Press, 2001.

Jamieson, Kathleen H. *Eloquence in an Electronic Age: The Transformation of Political Speechmaking.* New York: Oxford University Press, 1988.

Johnson, Benjamin. "Wilderness Parks and Their Discontents," In *American Wilderness: A New History,* edited by Michael Lewis, 113–130. Oxford: Oxford University Press, 2007.

Juergens, George. *News From the White House.* Chicago: The University of Chicago Press, 1981.

Kernell, Samuel. *Going Public: News Strategies of Presidential Leadership,* 3rd ed. Washington, D. C.: Congressional Quarterly Inc., 1997.

Laracey, Melvin C. *Presidents and the People: The Partisan Story of Going Public.* College Station: Texas A&M University Press, 2002.

Lears, T. J. Jackson. *No Place of Grace: Antimodernism and the Transformation of American Culture, 1880–1920.* New York: Pantheon Books, 1981.

Levi-Strauss, Claude. *The Savage Mind.* Chicago: The University of Chicago Press, 1966.

Lincoln, Bruce. *Discourse and the Construction of Society: Comparative Studies of Myth, Ritual, and Classification.* New York: Oxford University Press, 1989.

Lucas, Stephen E. "George Washington and the Rhetoric of Presidential Leadership." In *The*

Presidency and Rhetorical Leadership, edited by Leroy G. Dorsey, 42–72. College Station: Texas A&M University Press, 2002.

Lutts, Ralph H. *The Nature Fakers: Wildlife, Science & Sentiment*. Charlottesville: The University Press of Virginia, 2001.

McGee, W. J. *Proceeding of a Conference of Governors in the White House, Washington, D. C., May 13–15, 1908*. New York: Arno Press, 1972.

McGerr, Michael. *A Fierce Discontent: The Rise and Fall of the Progressive Movement in America, 1870–1920*. Oxford: Oxford University Press, 2003.

Marsh, George P. *Man and Nature*. Edited by David Lowenthal. Cambridge: The Belknap Press of Harvard University Press, 1965.

Medhurst, Martin J. "Afterword: The Ways of Rhetoric." In *Before the Rhetorical Presidency*, edited by Martin J. Medhurst, 329–334. College Station: Texas A&M University Press, 2008.

———. "Introduction—A Tale of Two Constructs: The Rhetorical Presidency Versus Presidential Rhetoric." In *Beyond the Rhetorical Presidency*, edited by Martin J. Medhurst, xi-xxv. College Station: Texas A&M University Press, 1996.

———. "Was There a Nineteenth-Century Rhetorical Presidency? A Debate Revisited." In *Before the Rhetorical Presidency*, edited by Martin J. Medhurst, 1–16. College Station: Texas A&M University Press, 2008.

Merchant, Carolyn. *American Environmental History: An Introduction*. New York: Columbia University Press, 2007.

Milkis, Sidney M. *Theodore Roosevelt, the Progressive Party, and the Transformation of American Democracy*. Lawrence: University Press of Kansas, 2009.

Miller, Char. *Gifford Pinchot and the Making of Modern Environmentalism*. Washington: Island Press, 2001.

Morris, Edmund. *Theodore Rex*. New York: Random House, 2001.

Nash, Roderick F. "The Conservation Impulse, Beginnings—1878." In *American Environmentalism: Readings in Conservation History*, edited by Roderick F. Nash, 3rd ed., 9–11. New York: McGraw-Hill, Inc., 1990.

Nash, Roderick F., *Wilderness and the American Mind*, 4th ed. New Haven: Yale University Press, 2001.

Opie, John. *Nature's Nation: An Environmental History of the United States*. Fort Worth: Harcourt Brace College Publishers, 1998.

Oravec, Christine. "Conservationism vs. Preservationism: The 'Public Interest' in the Hetch Hetchy Controversy." *Quarterly Journal of Speech* 70 (1984): 444–458.

Perelman, Chaim, and L. Olbrechts-Tyteca. *The New Rhetoric: A Treatise on Argumentation*. Translated by John Wilkinson and Purcell Weaver. Notre Dame: University of Notre Dame Press, 1969.

Perreault, Melanie. "American Wilderness and First Contact." In *American Wilderness: A New History*, edited by Michael Lewis, 15–34. Oxford: Oxford University Press, 2007.

Pinchot, Gifford. *Breaking New Ground*. New York: Harcourt, Brace and Company, 1947.

———. *The Fight for Conservation*. Seattle: University of Washington Press, 1910.

Plazak, Dan. *A Hole in the Ground with a Liar at the Top: Fraud and Deceit in the Golden Age of American Mining*. Salt Lake City: The University of Utah Press, 2006.

Ponder, Stephen. "Federal News Management in the Progressive Era: Gifford Pinchot and the Conservation Crusade." *Journalism History* 13.2 (1986): 42–48.

———. "'Publicity in the Interest of the People': Theodore Roosevelt's Conservation Crusade." *Presidential Studies Quarterly* 20.3 (1990): 547–555.

Richardson, Elmo R. *The Politics of Conservation: Crusades and Controversies, 1897–1913*. Berkeley: University of California Press, 1962.

Robertson, James O. *American Myth, American Reality*. New York: Hill & Wang, 1980.

Roosevelt, Theodore. *An Autobiography*. New York: Charles Scribner's Sons, 1929.

———. "Annual Message, January 2, 1899." In *State Papers as Governor and President 1899–1909*. The Works of Theodore Roosevelt, National Edition, vol. XV, 5–29. New York: Charles Scribner's Sons, 1926.

———. "Annual Message, January 3, 1900." In *State Papers as Governor and President 1899–1909*. The Works of Theodore Roosevelt, National Edition, vol. XV, 30–76. New York: Charles Scribner's Sons, 1926.

———. "At a Meeting of the Society of American Foresters, Held at the Residence of Mr. Gifford Pinchot, Washington, D. C., March 26, 1903." In *Presidential Addresses and State Paper*, Homeward Bound Edition, volume I, 249–257. New York: The Review of Reviews Company, 1910.

———. "At Cairo, Ill., October 3, 1907." In *Presidential Addresses and State Papers*, Homeward Bound Edition, Volume VI, 1405–1419. New York: The Review of Reviews Company, 1910.

———. "At St. Louis, MO., October 2, 1907." In *Presidential Addresses and State Papers*, Homeward Bound Edition, Volume VI, 1390–1405. New York: The Review of Reviews Company, 1910.

———. "Before the National Editorial Association at Jamestown, VA., June 10, 1907." In *Presidential Addresses and State Papers*, Homeward Bound Edition, Volume VI, 1308–1323. New York: The Review of Reviews Company, 1910.

———. *California Addresses by President Roosevelt.* San Francisco: The California Promotion Committee, 1903.

———. "First Annual Message (1901)." In *State Papers as Governor and President 1899–1909*. The Works of Theodore Roosevelt, National Edition, vol. XV, 81–138. New York: Charles Scribner's Sons, 1926.

———. "Forestry and Business." in *American Problems*, in The Works of Theodore Roosevelt, National Edition, vol. XVI, 100–108. New York: Charles Scribner's Sons, 1926.

———. "Message Communicated to the Two House of Congress, February 13, 1907." In *Presidential Addresses and State Paper*, Homeward Bound Edition, volume VI, 1145–1164. New York: The Review of Reviews Company, 1910.

———. *Ranch Life and the Hunting-Trail.* Lincoln: University of Nebraska Press, 1983.

———. "The Campaign Against Privilege, January 31, 1908." In *The Roosevelt Policy: Speeches, Letters and State Papers, related to Corporate Wealth and Closely Allied Topics*, edited by William Griffith, volume 2, 705–745. New York: Kraus Reprint Co., 1971.

———. *The Wilderness Hunter*; *Outdoor Pastimes of an American Hunte*r. In The Works of Theodore Roosevelt, National Edition, vol. XV. New York: Charles Scribner's Sons, 1926.

———. *The Winning of the West: An Account of the Exploration and Settlement of Our Country from the Alleghanies to the Pacific.* In the Works of Theodore Roosevelt, National Edition, vols. VIII & IX. New York: Charles Scribner's Sons, 1926.

———. "To the Deep Waterway Convention at Memphis, Tenn., October 4, 1907." In *Presidential Addresses and State Papers*, Homeward Bound Edition, Volume VI, 1419–1442. New York: The Review of Reviews Company, 1910.

———. *Through the Brazilian Wilderness and Papers on Natural History*. In the Works of Theodore Roosevelt, National Edition, vol. V. New York: Charles Scribner's Sons, 1926.

———. "To the School Children of the United States, April 15, 1907." In *Presidential Addresses and State Paper*, Homeward Bound Edition, volume VI, 1207–1213. New York: The Review of Reviews Company, 1910.

Rosenzweig, Roy. *Eight Hours for What We Will: Workers & Leisure in an Industrial City, 1870–1920.* Cambridge: Cambridge University Press, 1987.

Rushing, Janice H. "The Rhetoric of the American Western Myth." *Communication Monographs* 50.1 (1983): 14–32.

Saldin, Robert P. "William McKinley and the Rhetorical Presidency." *Presidential Studies Quarterly* 41.1 (2011): 119–134.

Senecah, Susan. "Forever Wild or Forever in Battle: Metaphors of Empowerment in the Continuing Controversy over the Adirondacks." In *EarthTalk: Communication Empowerment for Environmental Action*, edited by Star A. Muir and Thomas L. Veenendall, 95–118. Westport: Praeger, 1996.

Sheffield, Jessica. "Theodore Roosevelt, 'Conservation as a National Duty.'" *Voices of Democracy* 5 (2010): 89–108.

Shepherd, Jack. *The Forest Killers: The Destruction of the American Wilderness*. New York: Weybright and Talley, 1975.

Slotkin, Richard. *Gunfighter Nation: The Myth of the Frontier in Twentieth-Century America*. New York: Atheneum, 1992.

———. *Regeneration Through Violence: The Mythology of the American Frontier, 1600–1860*. Norman: University of Oklahoma Press, 1973.

———. *The Fatal Environment: The Myth of the Frontier in the Age of Industrialization, 1800–1890*. Norman: University of Oklahoma Press, 1998.

Smith, Frank E. *The Politics of Conservation*. New York: Pantheon Books, 1966.

Smith, Henry N. *Virgin Land: The American West as Symbol and Myth*. Cambridge: Harvard University Press, 1978.

Stedman, Raymond W. *Shadows of the Indian: Stereotypes in American Culture*. Norman: University of Oklahoma Press, 1982.

Steinberg, Ted. *Down to Earth: Nature's Role in American History*, 3rd ed. Oxford: Oxford University Press, 2013.

Stoll, Steven. "Farm Against Forest." In *American Wilderness: A New History*, edited by Michael Lewis, 55–72. Oxford: Oxford University Press, 2007.

Stuckey, Mary. "Establishing the Rhetorical Presidency through Presidential Rhetoric: Theodore Roosevelt and the Brownsville Raid." *Quarterly Journal of Speech* 92.3 (2006): 287–309.

Taylor, Alan. "'Wasty Ways': Stories of American Settlement." In *American Environmental History*, edited by Louis S. Warren, 102–118. Malden: Blackwell Publishing, 2003.

Tulis, Jeffrey K. *The Rhetorical Presidency*. Princeton: Princeton University Press, 1987.

White, James B. *When Words Lose Their Meaning: Constitutions and Reconstitutions of Language, Character, and Community*. Chicago: The University of Chicago Press, 1984.

Wyant, William K. *Westward in Eden: The Public Lands and the Conservation Movement*. Berkeley: University of California Press, 1982.

Zarefsky, David. "The Presidency Has Always Been a Place for Rhetorical Leadership." In *The Presidency and Rhetorical Leadership*, edited by Leroy G. Dorsey, 20–41. College Station: Texas A&M University Press, 2002.

Index

CPSIA information can be obtained
at www.ICGtesting.com
Printed in the USA
FSOW02n0830110316
17897FS

9 781623 493998